Praise for *Wild Magic*

"Like a weaving of the winds or the many-fea[...] *Wild Magic* is an inspired blending of folk practice, mystical scholarship that draws upon the rich cultural heritage of the British Isles, Ireland, and Gaul. Informed by ancient lore, and grounded in Celtic customs by the inclusion of traditional chants, prayers, and spells, Danu Forest presents clear tools and workings that guide the modern seeker along the path to personal relationship with the land, its spirits, and the Gods and guardians of place. This work is a love letter that gathers together authentic information about what the various Celtic peoples believed and practiced, as well as an invitation to put that understanding to respectful use in order to traverse the wild and hidden places both within us and without."

—Jhenah Telyndru, author of *Avalon Within*
and *The Mythic Moons of Avalon*

"Danu Forest invites us on an immersive journey into the Celtic Otherworld. She has deftly interwoven both the practical and the magical, leading the reader towards an authentic alignment with the wild magic of the land itself. Through spells, exercises, guided journeys and folklore from the Celtic traditions, Forest shows us how to reclaim our connection to our own wildness and live in accordance with the spirit of place, wherever we call home. Forest has written a beautiful compendium that is especially poignant in a time when many long for a return to a meaningful sense of relationship with the wild."

—Danielle Blackwood, author of *The Twelve Faces of the Goddess*

"*Wild Magic* is an invaluable compendium of old country lore that we are desperate for today, and Danu's voice brings a deep knowledge born of impeccable research and dedicated practice infused with the enticement to dance on the wild side … To feel embraced by Earth, to dive deep into Water, to be uplifted by Air as well as engaging in soul-stirring practices like 'how to capture the wind' or 'how to read the web' and heart-warming lore like 'the kindling prayer' and 'the Woodcutter's Song.' A practical and magical elemental map to the immanent, *Wild Magic* is a powerful call to bring back the flow of nature to nurture our spirits and uplift our souls. Highly, highly recommended, especially to anyone working with the cycle of the seasons. Bring back the wild! Danu shows us how."

—Tiffany Lazic, author of *The Great Work: Self-Knowledge and Healing Through the Wheel of the Year*

"*Wild Magic* is a rich and practical compendium for working magic within the natural world."

—Philip Carr-Gomm, author of *Druid Mysteries*

WILD
MAGIC

About the Author

Danu Forest is a traditional Celtic wisewoman who has studied on the Celtic path for more than thirty years. She is noted for her many years of experience, her gifts as a natural hereditary seer, and her scholarlyresearch. She lives in the wild marshes surrounding the legendary Glastonbury Tor in the UK and works deeply with traditional lore as well as plant spirits, ancestors, and the powers of the land. Danu has been teaching for nearly twenty years and runs courses as well as online workshops and a magical and healing consultancy. She is the author of several books, including Celtic Tree Magic: Ogham Lore and Druid Mysteries, and she holds an MA in Celtic Studies, specializing in the Celtic Otherworld and traditional Celtic magic. Visit her online at www.DanuForest .co.uk.

To Write to the Author

If you wish to contact the author or would like more information about this book, please write to the author in care of Llewellyn Worldwide Ltd. and we will forward your request. Both the author and publisher appreciate hearing from you and learning of your enjoyment of this book and how it has helped you. Llewellyn Worldwide Ltd. cannot guarantee that every letter written to the author can be answered, but all will be forwarded. Please write to:

Danu Forest
℅ Llewellyn Worldwide
2143 Wooddale Drive
Woodbury, MN 55125-2989
Please enclose a self-addressed stamped envelope for reply,
or $1.00 to cover costs. If outside the U.S.A., enclose
an international postal reply coupon.

Many of Llewellyn's authors have websites with additional
information and resources. For more information,
please visit our website at http://www.llewellyn.com

WILD
MAGIC

Celtic
Folk
Traditions
for the
Solitary
Practitioner

DANU FOREST

Llewellyn Publications
Woodbury, Minnesota

FIRST EDITION
Seventh Printing, 2023

Book design by Samantha Peterson
Cover design by Kevin R. Brown
Editing by Laura Kurtz
Interior illustrations by Dan Goodfellow

Llewellyn Publications is a registered trademark of Llewellyn Worldwide Ltd.

Library of Congress Cataloging-in-Publication Data
Names: Forest, Danu, author.
Title: Wild magic : Celtic folk traditions for the solitary practitioner /
  Danu Forest.
Description: First edition. | Woodbury, Minnesota : Llewellyn Publications,
  [2020] | Includes bibliographical references and index. | Summary:
  "Celtic-based natural magical practices; incl. mythology, botanical
  information"—Provided by publisher.
Identifiers: LCCN 2020030011 (print) | LCCN 2020030012 (ebook) | ISBN
  9780738762678 (paperback) | ISBN 9780738763590 (ebook)
Subjects: LCSH: Magic, Celtic. | Faery-Faith (Wiccan sect) | Nature
  worship. | Mythology, Celtic. | Nature—Mythology—Ireland.
Classification: LCC BF1622.C45 F67 2020 (print) | LCC BF1622.C45 (ebook)
  | DDC 133.4/3089916—dc23
LC record available at https://lccn.loc.gov/2020030011
LC ebook record available at https://lccn.loc.gov/2020030012

Llewellyn Publications
A Division of Llewellyn Worldwide Ltd.
2143 Wooddale Drive
Woodbury, MN 55125-2989
www.llewellyn.com

Printed in the United States of America

For my family
of both blood and spirit
and all the other wild things of the forest.

CONTENTS

PRACTICALS AND EXERCISES

Disclaimer

The wild is wonderful, but it can also be dangerous, even with all the knowledge and experience in the world. In this book you may discover all sorts of techniques and resources to help you explore the wild and wild Celtic spirituality in its various forms, but it is essential that any knowledge found in any book goes hand in hand with your own common sense, careful preparation, and awareness of the practical risks inherent in any particular location or situation. It is important to always be fully responsible for our own welfare and those around us when in wild places. We need to be careful of wild weather and not to take risks when engaging spiritually with storms or high winds; equally, we need to know fire regulations in national parks, and take care for the fire safety of all life forms around us. We must be fully knowledgeable and responsible about any plants we may inhale or ingest and let people know our plans before disappearing into wild places for any length of time. Guides, food, water, safety, and communication equipment—especially first aid kits and phones—are irreplaceable in many wild places. In every endeavour, we need to remember that safety is always first.

Acknowledgements

No book is ever written alone, and my deep gratitude goes to all those who have helped me along the way: to my teachers, students, and fellow travellers, and especially to Dan Goodfellow for his unwavering support and beautiful illustrations, and to the team at Llewellyn, most notably Elysia Gallo and Laura Kurtz for making this book the best it can be.

Introduction
WHAT IS WILD MAGIC?

Feel the air in your lungs and your feet upon the ground. Feel your heart beating. Underneath the everyday, our daily concerns, and cultural routines, each of us is wild inside. We are every one of us living on this earth with the land beneath us, and the sun moon and stars above. Every one of us needs clean air, clean water, and good food. Every one of us has a long line of ancestors who walked this earth before us; they faced similar challenges, highs and lows, and lived in a world as full of the potential for spiritual connection as any one of us today. My ancestors, the Celts of Britain and Ireland, are often said to have lived in closer communion with the earth and venerated nature in a way seldom seen in the modern era. However, the earth and spirits who dwell within and upon this earth are as accessible to us today as ever. What has changed is not nature or the spirit world but *us*—clothed in our technology and plastic and concrete cities, it is we who live with the delusion that we are somehow distanced from nature, from the wild, and the effects of our behaviour towards it. The wild has never truly left; it is we who have merely closed our eyes and pretended to leave it far behind.

1

We are, each of us, wild, if we strip away the conditioning and conventions that force us to change our shape to live with the constraints of the modern world. We can see *wild* as a negative or even frightening term these days, as it comes with a host of associations we find hard to control—instinctual, unconstrained, fierce, even, and driven by an inner voice or calling that pays no heed to the rules which govern our societies. *Wild* has also become something we quietly admire, or even treasure as something outside ourselves, as if it were something inaccessible, something which has no place in this world even while we mourn its loss. We see a nobility in wild things, a presence, a power, while at the same time we partake in a culture which strips the wild away without mercy, destroying habitats and all the life forms that rely on them with endless hunger. Our consumerist lifestyle strives to take more and more for itself to fill a void within each of us—a void made by our movement away from the wild within ourselves for which there is no compensation. Without the wild, without nature in all its diversity, we lose ourselves—not only our souls and our spiritual connection to our own presence here in the world, but ultimately our lives as a species. We cannot sever our connection to the whole of life.

When we separate from nature, when we strive to trim and tame it, we separate from our own inner natures and ultimately the spirit world as well. Our inner calling, our inner connection, our inner voice, that access to the unknowable *All* that enlivens our eyes and vivifies and enflames our hearts dims to failing embers and we become sterile as dust. It is when we shift our awareness and honour our innate physicality and animal presence in this world as one among many that something shifts. We can open our awareness to something far greater than ourselves once again. Without words or doctrine, without rules that come from outside ourselves, we may instead access an inner knowing or sense of guidance that comes from both a wider, deeper source than anything we can comprehend, and at the same moment is something that dances in our veins and sits in our human bellies saying *This!* with the roar of lions and crashing waves, as sure as the heat of a fire or the blazing sun. We know in our bones and our beating hearts how to navigate this life with honour, nobility, and inner truth as human animals and bodies in space and time. In the same moment, we are also infinite spirits, ageless as the skies above. Like caged birds, when we tame our spirits and our lives, we lose something precious, something vital within us that gives us meaning beyond words. When we reconnect, miracles can happen. We can gently blow those embers back to a blaze and can find ourselves to be far more than we ever realised, living in an infinite universe, full of life. Full of magic.

Animism, the belief that all things have a spirit and life within them no matter how different from our own, allows our awareness to stretch beyond the merely physical and material and our consciousness to strive beyond a human centric version of the universe into something far larger. Religions and spiritual paths of all kinds strive to define this greater *All* and guide our connection with it, clothing it in a myriad of names and stories, but none of us need do anything other than step outside, feel the wind on our faces, listen to that little voice inside that pulls us to the woods or the shore, and be with it—*really* be with it for the healing and the reconnection to happen. Our connection with the gods and the infinite by any and all names was always there, merely forgotten for a moment. Our connection is as much a part of us as the blood in our veins and the air in our lungs. It is everywhere. It is wild, and so are we.

In this book you will find two threads woven together: practical lore and country wisdom coming from Celtic tradition and common sense or knowledge of things that work together with something more subtle, a passing on of old magic. Many of the old spells and charms of our ancestors have not survived, and yet so many have; it's important to remember that it is not the spells or the form that matters most, it is the connection with the spirits and powers of place that truly matter. All magic in the Celtic traditions ultimately comes of this relationship with spirit, the nurturing of friendship with the faerie folk, the green kin, the trees and plants, the ancestors, and the very land itself. We are required to be a living fusion of animal and eternal, here and grounded, manifest on this earth here and now, and able to walk hand in hand with our spirit cousins, those who walk unseen. It requires us to be able to access that deep knowing within ourselves, and the knowledge of who we are, our ancestors, the roots that grow deep into the earth herself. It requires of us that we shake off our city eyes and acknowledge our wild selves once again.

Where it is possible to pass on a spell or other practice with its roots in our history I endeavour to do so as accurately and with as much honour to tradition as I am able, noting specific origins and heritage within the wider Celtic cultures wherever I can. Equally, however, as someone who has spent three decades working with this land beneath my feet and studying the practices of those who came before me to a great depth practically spiritually and academically, I feel that our magic comes as much from our present connection to the spirits and the land as it does from our traditions. Where something has not survived, I see no difficulty in being re-inspired and creating my own magic, following the prompting of my faery friends, familiars, and other spirit kin. Indeed, the many Celtic nations of Britain, the Isle of Man, Brittany, and Ireland, along the Atlantic coast and northern Europe always had their differences (and similarities) and continue to do so. This is a living and wide-ranging tradition or collection of tradition; it is not in need of taming with organised systems, or excusing for the lack of them.

Helping Spirits: Gods, Familiars, Guardians, and Allies

In many of the practical exercises in the pages ahead, you'll see it advised to call in your guardians and allies. These may take any form—for example, gods you may choose to honour; ancestral spirits; traditional familiars; and faerie, animal, or other spirit allies. This book is suitable for beginners to this subject as well as those with more experience who wish to delve deeper into this style of practice. Central to this work is a close connection with spirits, but that connection in no way depends on having psychic skills, or *the Sight* as it's known in Celtic cultures. Instead, that connection requires us to build positive relationships with these beings and seek to strengthen our inner vision, our main means of establishing contact.

We call in allies or familiars not because what we do is inherently dangerous (although all work with the spirits should be treated with care) but because our indigenous traditions and magic rely on this connection with the otherworld. The magic we practice depends on a collective and recipro-cal relationship with those who dwell there. Together we become greater than the sum of our parts, and a sense of connection is seen in every layer of the practice—from our spiritual development to our practical magic to our everyday lives and the relationship with our environment.

If you already work with spirits and have guides and allies of any form, feel free to call them in to assist you with the practices suggested here. If this is new to you, be aware that this is not as difficult nor as deep water as it sounds!

We all have spirit allies, even if we are not aware of them. Calling these allies and asking for their help is the best way to begin to notice their sup-port. A spirit ally could be an ancestor or another spirit who agreed before your birth to support you, and whether their benevolent care is something we may only be aware of fleetingly or something we call on daily, they are always there. We all tend to call in spiritual assistance at certain times of our lives, and this is no different; a simple "Please help!" will do the trick. If you feel attracted to work with a Celtic deity this is a good opportunity to begin calling them into your life; it could be as simple as asking, for exam-ple, "Dear Brigid, please come to me here, thank you!" Equally, if you are used to working with animal spirits or faeries, they can be asked to help you, too.

Exercises to find allies related to the land, the air, the water, and the fire are included in this book, as are exercises to help you find animal allies and your familiars. I encourage you to try the exercises in the order presented for the best results.

Journeying, Inner Vision, and Guided Meditations

Throughout this book you will be taken on numerous journeys and guided meditations to help you connect with various spirit beings. All the exercises in this book are completely safe and can be used exactly as they are for an effective experience. The elements in these journeys all draw from tradi-tional imagery and as such function as energetic "keys" to help the psyche to access other levels of reality and other spirit destinations. Such was the purposes of many teaching tales in the Celtic tradition which have survived to the modern era and the details within them that may seem archaic or hard to understand rationally. In this sense, the journey and meditation pathways in this book attempt to recreate the effects drawn from the traditional tales and accounts of the Celtic mystical experience for the modern period. However, everyone is different and at different parts of their spiritual path or magical path; as such, these journeys should be taken as guides or templates only. There is no attempt here to define or dictate a seeker's spiritual experience or define those spirit beings that may be encountered but rather to provide a training example that can be developed, adapted, or discarded at will. Some will find they are only able to engage with these journeys using their imaginations, and the experience will stay within the seeker's mind until sufficient practice has been undertaken to allow them to go deeper. That is fine; the imagination is a powerful tool to help us translate the spirit realm and its communications, so experiences at this level are still immensely valuable. Others with previous experience or steady practice will find themselves able to move beyond their own minds and experience a genuine change of consciousness for the duration—this is completely safe and is the aim of seership and animist or shamanic experience. Others may find these guides to be useful starting off points from which they may explore the energies concerned independently.

What you see or experience may or may not match the descriptions I have given them, and this is perfectly fine and to be expected. Things in the spirit realm do not always appear in the same way every time, for anyone, and there is no substitute for genuine connection and interaction, which will be of greater importance than anything you may read in any book. Journeying and seership takes a great deal of practice for most people, and the thing to look out for is the subtle shift of awareness, the felt sensation in your belly, or the sense that time has shifted in a way different from your every day. One of the deepest experiences in fact often go beyond words or any visual details, where the seeker experiences a deep shift of awareness with very little happening which can be described, or even a sense that nothing happened at all, other than a change of feeling. This is perhaps the deepest level of connection of all; moving beyond one's rational mind entirely into a wider communion with the spirit realm.

Every journey will mention calling in your guides and allies (known sometimes as the *co-choisitche* or the "the one who walks with you" in Scots Gaelic) and any protection, before you begin. While these exercises are safe, it is always sensible to call in assistance from the spirit realm beforehand and create some form of sacred boundaries in your physical location. The spirit realm is not there merely for our entertainment or exploration, and many beings of all descriptions may be found there. Indeed, it is not even one singular destination but many—the approach should be similar to any period of travel: with a guide, awareness of the terrain, enough resources and precautions to ensure your welfare, and a sense of confident and enthusiastic but grounded curiosity.

Words from the Bards: Traditional Tales

Throughout this book are numerous traditional tales, sayings, poems, and songs. In most cases these are direct reproductions with references for those who wish to seek their sources. On other occasions I have collated versions of a tale and re-told it in my own words for clarity or as translation. In every instance the source of these tales is noted in the footnotes to honour their source cultures within the broader Celtic nations, as well as where possible those who originally recorded them. Celts were and still are great tellers of tales that teach as well as entertain, and every instance of this practice is a treasure in its own right that provides examples of the culture as well as the beliefs and practices situated within them. To discuss a Celtic belief or practice without an example of its accompanying tale where there is one would be remiss, so they are included here with all the honour they deserve as wisdom teachings, and to provide wonder for the soul.

One

AN CREIDEAMH SÍ: THE CELTIC FAERY FAITH

Throughout this book we'll be looking at what is commonly termed "Celtic" magical and spiritual lore. When we discuss the Celts, we are really using an umbrella term for a group of Iron Age tribes around northern and western Europe and the Atlantic fringe, and later into the modern period, a group of Celtic speaking nations with widely different heritages despite shared cultural roots that stem from a common group of languages and beliefs. There are differences between these nations that are important to recognise and honour. Ideas of the otherworld and the spirit realm vary across time and geography, as does the location of the spirit realm and any cosmological systems accompanying it, even as the common threads of belief may be traced within them. However, those common threads are substantial and have endured. Where there is difference, there is also cohesion; where there is unity, there is also uniqueness between each country and throughout the eras and time spans discussed. I aim to acknowledge both.

One of the earliest records of the Celts' views of the gods come from the accounts of the writer Diodorus Siculus of the war leader Brennus on a visit to the Greek sanctuary at Delphi in the first century BCE:

> Brennus, the king of the Gauls, on entering a temple found
> no dedications of gold or silver, and when he came only upon
> images of stone and wood he laughed at them, to think that
> men, believing that gods have human form, should set up their
> images in wood and stone.[1]

At least at this early stage before the Roman Conquest, it seems the
Celts believed that the gods did not take human forms but were instead
considered present and immanent in the world around them without the
need for anthropomorphism. There was no reason to constrain any understanding of them by limiting them with human bodies and human ways.
While this perspective undoubtedly changed over time—indeed, Celtic art
of later periods abound with humanlike depictions of the gods—the initial
principle remained; the gods are everywhere in nature and are the natural
forces themselves. The human world is part of an infinite whole, but it is
neither its centre nor its periphery. The gods are part of nature, in a vast
multiplicity of being, far beyond our comprehension. They are wild things,
and we with them.

The same conceptualization can be seen in the Celtic ideas about death,
that each soul would travel to the otherworld but that death was part of an
endless cycle of life impossible to separate from and thus not the final end
or to be feared, but understood to be integral to our very being. Trust in the
greater cycle of life was a guiding principle of the Celts, and according to the
Romans, played a huge part in the famed Celtic bravery and individualism.

> And you, ye druids... Your teaching is that the shades of the
> dead do not make their way to the silent abode of Erebus or
> the lightless realm of Dis below, but that the same soul ani-
> mates the limbs in another sphere. If you sing of certainties,
> death is the centre of continuous life... happy in their error,
> for they are not harassed by the greatest of terrors, the fear of

---

1. Diodorus Siculus, *Library of History, Volume XI: Fragments of Books 21-32,* trans. Francis R. Walton. (Cambridge, MA: Loeb Classical Library. Harvard University Press, 1957), 146.

death. This gives the warrior his eagerness to rush upon the /
steel, a spirit ready to face death, and an indifference to save a
life which will return.[2]

LUCAN, PHARSALIA, BOOK I, LINES 450–462

Just as wild nature, we all live, we all die, and life continues.

Discussing the wild with regard to the Celts, it's important to note that
these were highly civilised people who traded widely; they were magnificent
craftsmen, scholars, and philosophers as well as warriors and mysterious, mystical druids. While they had no written language of their own, they traded and
travelled widely, many were proficient in several languages, and they had a rich
culture of storytelling and advanced spiritual thought, as well as mathematics
and astronomical observation—as attested to in the magnificent Coligny calendar. They had a culture equal in sophistication to the Greeks who wrote of
them and the Romans who eventually conquered them. However, they also
had a love of the land—an awe at the power of nature that placed the honouring of the wild at the centre of their awareness. Animals and sacred trees held
special importance in their local communities, which continued under Roman
rule, and is a practice which continues to this day, in a multitude of forms. The
wild and the sophisticated are not sperate in Celtic culture; one springs from
the other like blossoms upon a tree.

In the later Christian period, the Celtic belief in spirits and even the old
gods remained, changed and adapted by a phenomenon called *syncretism*—
people found a way to be Christian and even attend church while holding the
beliefs in the old ways simultaneously. The *Creideamh Sí* (Irish) or the faery
faith continued well into the modern era and is still found in various forms
across Ireland and Scotland. In a development somewhat unique to Celtic
lands, the old ways and old gods transposed into a Christian worldview;
[Christian scholars of the time] wrote in the belief that the old gods were
merely fallen angels expelled from heaven but not bad enough for hell, and
thus became the faerie folk. As such, practices honouring them and working

---

2. Lucan, *Pharsalia, Book 1, lines 450–62*, trans. Nora K. Chadwick, *The Druids* (Cardiff, Wales,
  UK: University of Wales Press, 1966), 53–54.

with them were not considered evil or taboo.[3] Records from the Scottish witch trials attest that those who worked with the faeries were usually considered good people, cunning men or women who practiced good magic, as opposed to "witches" who would be said to work with the devil.[4] While such categories proved to be largely arbitrary in practice and terms like *faery* and *demon* were often used interchangeably, a belief in the unseen, that the spirits and the old gods resided still in the wild hills, continued into the modern era and survive to this day. That these beings still needed honouring and could be called upon for help, maintained a pattern of magical and spiritual practice with its roots going back perhaps thousands of years.

The cycles of the seasons and the sun and moon, which are often marked out in the alignments of British and Irish stone circles and other Neolithic monuments, also form a structure of celebration and ritual connection with the land. These observances continued through the Celtic Iron Age, into the Anglo-Saxon period, and later into the Medieval Celtic liturgical calendar of saint's days and other events that often merged the old Pagan feast days into the new Christian faith. These seasonal celebrations were intimately connected with the agricultural yearly cycle, but also infused the practical with the spiritual; each season was seen to have its spirits and overarching deities or saints, and where once druids oversaw fire ceremonies at the cross-quarter days of Imbolc, Beltane, Lughnasadh, and Samhain, now the priest led the community in ritual blessings and services at Candle Mass, Mayday, Lammas or Harvest festival, and All Hallows Eve. Where once the Goddess Brighid was asked to bless the hearths and the livestock, now it was Saint Brigit, the midwife of Christ. But the rituals, the dates of the festivals and the wisdom behind them remained. They were still, as they say in Welsh, *Ysbrydnos*—spirit nights.

With those spirit nights, those old practices, surviving across hundreds and perhaps thousands of years, comes a host of charms and spells, simple

---

3. John Carey, "The Old Gods of Ireland," *Understanding Celtic Religion: Revisiting the Pagan Past* (Cardiff, Wales, UK: University of Wales Press, 2015), 65.

4. Emma Wilby, *Cunning Folk and Familiar Spirits: Shamanistic Visionary Traditions in Early Modern British Witchcraft and Magic* (East Sussex, UK: Sussex Academic Press, 2013), 26.

ritual practices and folkloric wisdom, merged and woven with a deep practical knowledge of the land and all its inhabitants. The Celtic lore of both animal and spirit forms in addition to the deep instinctual knowing of the Genius Loci (the powers of place or the old ones who give a land its identity or soul) has remained, evolved, grown, and made suitable for each new generation for each of us to come to anew. The wild continues to ignite our spirits and nourish our souls.

A "Celtic" Cosmology

To the ancient Gauls, the spirit realm was both a terrestrial location as well as a spiritual one. Found over the sea and sometimes described as residing on the island of Britain itself, the Gauls shared a common language with tribes on the southern coast of Britain. The seat and origin of their religion was described as residing in Britain, most likely on Anglesey.[5] However, they also maintained a belief that there were three realms: *Albios*, translated roughly as *the upper world*, or *the white* or *blessed world*; *Bitu, the land/ the world where we live*; and *Dubnos*, the *underworld* or *the deep place*. The later nineteenth-century Welsh antiquarian Iolo Morganwg established a cosmology of the three worlds which mirrored this system. *Gwynfyd*, meaning the *white life, the upperworld*; *Abred*, the middle realm; and *Annwfn, the underworld* or the *deep place*, plus *Ceugant, infinity/ the void*. While it is unclear whether Morgannwg's three-world system is as ancient as he claimed, it bears striking similarity to the Gaulish worldview and nonetheless has been taken up within modern Druidry. The term *Annwn*, or more accurately, *Annwfn*, etymologically drawn from the Gaulish *Dubnos*, is genuinely of very ancient origin, used as the generic name for the Welsh otherworld, and of the spirits as well as the land of the dead. In folklore as well as in the surviving literature Annwfn may be found in numerous ways, by crossing the sea or entering the depths of a lake, as well as by climbing to a high place, or entering the very earth itself, often via one of the hollow hills said to be the homes

---

5. Julius Caesar, *The Gallic Wars (Latin and English): De Bello Gallico*, trans. W. A. Macdevitt. (n.l.: Neptune Publishing, Kindle edition) location 6954 of 14665.

of the faerie folk. Equally the wanderer may stumble upon the Otherworld, unawares, or be sought out by its inhabitants and taken with them.

Triple Spiral Rock Carving

The otherworld in the Irish and Scottish traditions is interrelated as is their language. In Gaelic, the otherworld goes by many names and can be found in the same manner as in Welsh—over or under water or entering the earth. The otherworld is also found over the sea, on islands near the coast, or by an ocean voyage. In medieval Irish literature we can find the *Echtrai* and the *Immrama* tales; the Echtrai, literally meaning *adventure,* are pre-Christian in origin and concern the hero's journey into the otherworld and back via a sea voyage, or equally with a change in consciousness and state of mind. The later Immrama, also voyage tales, are Christian yet retain earlier Pagan motifs where the otherworld is found as an in-between state of neither earth nor heaven.

In this way we see the spirit world can be accessed in the mortal everyday world, and interaction with it always was and is considered to be something possible during the course of a normal life by the living *and* the dead. While ritual to access it was certainly undertaken, it was also understood to be reached via shifts in awareness, and even by mistake. It is both here, and elsewhere, simultaneously. The fact that the Gauls described the mortal world as part of an animistic or shamanic three-world system that could be navigated physically illustrates a belief in the spiritual dimension of the physical mortal world; the gods were immanent in nature and present around us at all times rather than residing in a distant and abstract location. It is for this reason that we are still able to access the spirits today and engage with them now with as much authenticity as at any point in the past.

The Aos Sí: Our Friends Beyond the Fields We Know

Integral to this work is connection with the spirits. In the various Celtic traditions these are usually seen as the faeries, but again this is a large umbrella term. Faeries go by many names in Gaelic or Celtic folklore and are seldom referred to directly in case it attracts their attention unwittingly. They are known in Ireland as the *Aos Sí*, Sidhe, or the Sith—otherworldly people of the Sidhe or *Sid* mounds, barrow and burial mounds of the Neolithic and Bronze age with which they are closely associated, and are often said to be the entrance to their homes. They are sometimes known as the *Daoine Sidhe* or *Daoine Maithe*, the *Good People*. In Scotland they are sometimes called the good neighbours or the Gentry as well as the Seelie and Unseelie Courts. They may dwell within aristocratic societies or as lone individuals, but often, especially in the Irish traditions, they are seen as lingering traces of the old pre-Christian gods, the Tuatha de Danann, as well as the vast spirit nations of the land who have dwelled in the land long before the humans came. Amongst the Sidhe may be found the dead, the ancestors, those recently passed, as well as those who travel between the worlds either willingly or as a result of faery abduction. The spirit world is never to be approached without caution and care, for while many spirits and faery beings there may be friendly, many others are not.

These beings are often seen as taller than humans (although this also varies), and their social structure seems to be broadly hierarchical, with kings and queens. In Wales, the faeries dwell in Annwfn, and equally go by several names, most commonly the Tylwyth Teg, and the Gwragedd Annwn. There are also vast numbers of other faerie races, some of which appear to have tribes while others are solitary. Some of these are attached to lakes, rivers, the sea, or to caves and old mines. Sometimes nature spirits are seen as part of the faerie realm, and certainly these exist as much as faeries, though they are more often found within the mortal world. Others are associated with particular trees or are considered companions and guardians to certain bloodlines, such as the *Bean Sidhe*, literally the *faery woman* who warns of an approaching death. The realms of the dead and those of faery often intertwine, and the ancestral spirits may also be found in the otherworld or transform into faery according to their own ways.

Many of our early witchcraft and folk magic traditions relied on the practitioner's connections with the faeries. Evidence such as the Scottish witch trial records show us that while the wider culture and state could be called Christian, in effect the numbers of people actually attending church was often relatively low, and when trouble struck, particularly in rural areas, people were often more likely to seek the help of a wise woman or cunning man with their faery helpers than the support of the clergy. Such practitioners were often said to have made pacts or arrangements with the king or queen of the faeries, who would assign them a helper who in turn would assist their magics and healing work. At other times, these people were said to have made pacts with the devil, but in practice the relationship and tone of the interaction seems to have been the same, and *the devil* and *the faeries* were often used interchangeably, as were the terms *wisewoman* and *witch*—such definitions as good and bad magical practitioners were entirely subjective and depended very much on a positive local reputation versus the accusations of enemies within the community.

The same ambiguous reputation can be seen in relation to the faeries themselves, who are known as able to be friendly or dangerous by turns. The Irish *Creideamh Sí* or *faery faith* goes back incredibly far. This faith revolves around negotiating the relationship with our otherworld kin to the best results, to include a series of taboos and careful etiquette to avoid offending the faeries, as well as traditions of propitiation to appease and garner friendship. While a faery friend can bestow great blessings, to offend the faeries is highly dangerous, and there are several examples concerning their revenge resulting in death, poverty, and madness not only to those who have offended them but to their whole bloodlines. Examples of faery revenge are known to still occur to this day, especially in Ireland and the Outer Hebrides.

Etiquette and Taboos

A key to working with faery is *respect*—these are our spirit nations, not sparkly little things from children's books. Our older folklore and faery tales have much to teach us about how to work with these beings. First and foremost, we must seek an ally to be a guide in this work who will negotiate with them for us and on our behalf. In spirit work of all kinds, allies are everything—they help us stay safe and navigate the otherworld and interactions with those we find there. We must also be grounded. This is work for robust people; being "away with the faeries" often means one has lost themselves and been enchanted by them. This does no good. Faeries are beings far closer to the soul of the world than we are, so it helps if we take on that earthy quality and apply a good dose of common sense to our practice. As well, be honest: you don't have to tell them everything or things you would prefer to keep private, but you must not lie. State clearly your intention and agree to nothing—make no pacts or deals until you are satisfied that you know exactly what the cost will be for the agreement. Another important aspect of etiquette and faery relations is the traditional taboo to not eat faery food. People find this difficult, but giving in always leads to trouble—ego inflation, glamouring (whereby a person becomes ungrounded and confused), and ultimately a loss of personal power, which means the end of any useful magical work or spiritual progression. Often the food is offered as something of a test, and people who succumb burn out their psychic and psychological fuses with serious results in their daily lives and to their mental health. So, take care—a taboo is a taboo for a reason! Next is iron—our connection with faeries is cut with iron, and all modern metals and technology seriously get in the way of useful, positive connection. Keep technology and metal away from your work with faeries, but privately make a mental note of where iron may be found in case you ever need to use it to sever an unfriendly faerie connection. For example, a horseshoe in your pocket is very useful. Finally are offerings. A traditional practice is to make our faery friends offerings such as gifts of cream, milk, butter, honey, or baked goods. These can be placed on an altar, or at a special place outside. Leave them there for a day or two before disposing; the faeries take the energy of the offering but what remains is not good for human consumption. Eating it would be rude and unhealthy, as all the life force has been taken from it. Make offerings regularly and generously to build and maintain relationships with your allies and faery kin.

Love of the Land

The land is in many ways the centre and heart of wild magic, for we are predominantly people of the earth. Until the most recent couple of generations, we lived in close relationship with the land, its seasons, and its moods and needs. As such, it was impossible for those who came before us to dismiss the sense that we are surrounded by spirits; they were understood to be in the ground beneath our feet, in the hills and mountains, in the tilled earth and wild wood, in rock and stone, roaming the land, and feasting within its hollow hills. The Welsh word for the otherworld, Annwfn, meaning *the deep place* is a spirit realm as easily accessed by travelling over sea, journeying beneath the lakes and rivers, or wandered into while walking on mortal soil. The deep place, the otherworld, is as much a different way of seeing the land, and accessing a different consciousness, as it is another physical place. For us to access this place, our awareness is what must change. This realm dwells beside us, beyond us, and within us, continually, from life to death and beyond.

It is in this otherworld that we may find the faerie folk, the Daoine Maithe, the Sidhe (Irish), the Tylwyth Teg (Welsh), the Elves (Scots and Saxon), An Lucht Sidhe, (Irish, *the shining ones*), the people of peace, as well as a host of other spirits. When considering the spiritual nature of the land itself, its often worth taking some time to really contemplate that just as we have souls or spirits, so does the land itself, and many beings who live here and share this earth with us have never had a physical form, yet are still dwelling in this realm in its spirit reality…not some distant spiritual plane. For just as the divine is immanent, fully present and indwelling here, so is all spirit, all life, in all its forms. It is but a hair's breadth away from our awareness, near enough to reach out and touch if we can slow down and reengage with our natural, wild selves.

Ways to Connect with the Faery Faith

Learn your tales and folk lore; these are rich stores of wisdom for dealing with the otherworld. Learn your land. Seeks places with faery folklore or that feel special to you. Walk in moonlight and at dawn and dusk, the liminal times of the day. Follow natures cycles, honour the wheel of the year. Eat local, seasonal food. Carry no iron or technology. Set up an altar or sacred space for communion with the spirits. Make offerings for the faeries and other spirits of baked goods, butter, and cream. Write or read poetry and the old tales, or music to share with your community. Recite your poems and tales or sing songs as offerings to the wild folk; even if you do not sense them, they are listening. Be patient. Walk gently through life. Be of open heart and mind. Call to them on the wind. One day, they will greet you as a friend.

The Land Spirits

There is a vast array of earth spirits and beings, faery folk and other wild things who walk between the otherworld and this mortal earth. They are found by experience, by noticing what others overlook, by seeking out quiet places, attending a piece of the land over time, and seeking friendship with the faery folk. Our myths, folklore, and legends are full of tales of those who have found them long before us, but they are actually still here, walking the land at dawn and dusk, dancing in the light and shadows of trees in the wind, sleeping in caves and mineshafts, and protecting our ancestors in their mounds and cairns.

Here is a list of just a few of the individual faery beings we may find out in the land:

The Knockers

The knockers are earth spirits closely associated with tin mines in Cornwall. They are said to show miners good loads of ore by flickering lights in the depths of the mine, and their knocking, from whence they get their name, was said to warn the miners of danger. Like all spirits, the knockers demand to be treated with respect or they will exact revenge, although they are kindly to those who leave offerings for them. In the past, miners would always leave a portion of their meal for the knockers in thanks for their friendship. But read on about a miner in Cornish folklore named Tom Trevorrow who crossed the knockers.

Traditional Tales
Tom Trevorrow (Cornish)

Tom Trevorrow, who when he was working underground heard the knockers just before him, and roughly told them "to be quiet and go." Upon which, a shower of stones fell suddenly around him, and gave him a dreadful fright. He seems however to have quickly got over it, and soon after, when eating his dinner, a number of squeaking voices sang:

Tom Trevorrow! Tom Trevorrow! Leave some of thy 'fuggan'[6] for bucca,[7] Or bad luck to thee to-morrow!

But Tom took no notice and ate up every crumb, upon which the knockers changed their song to:

Tommy Trevorrow! Tommy Trevorrow! We'll send thee bad luck to-morrow; Thou old curmudgeon, to eat all thy fuggan. And not leave a 'didjan'[8] for bucca.

---

6. Fuggan—A raisin cake popular with miners for their lunch.

7. Bucca—A trickster faery being, highly revered in Cornwall and here understood to be the leader of the knockers.

8. Didjan—A tiny bit or morsel of food. Here meaning not a scrap of cake, or an offering.

After this, such persistent ill-luck followed him that he was
obliged to leave the mine.[9]

The Bucca/ Bwca/ Pwca/ Pooka (Cornish/ Welsh/ Irish)

Sometimes understood as a pixie or other faerie being, the Bucca is also
revered as a god or powerful spirit by many Cornish witches. In Cornwall, the Bucca is sometimes seen as a kind of god or king of the faeries
or a leader of the knockers and should always be treated with great care.
Known as a shapeshifter and trickster, he may take several forms but is
often described as roughly humanoid with pointed features and completely
black or a fast-moving shadow over wild countryside.

The Glaistig

The Glaistig is commonly thought of as a tutelary spirit, one who oversees
a family or a patch of land. Her name comes from the Gaelic for grey, *glas*,
and she is usually described as a thin grey woman, with long fair hair and
a green dress. Sometimes she is called the *Green Glaistig (a Ghlaistig uaine)*,
her green dress denoting her faery nature. She is often said to have been
formerly a fine lady and mistress of the house, who had been taken into
faery and given a faery nature. She is said to take care of and offer protection especially to those who are foolish or weak willed, for she has great
strength although she will bring trouble to those who disrespect her. Like
the Bean Sidhe, she has a cry that can echo off the distant hills, announcing
times of joy or of sorrow upon the household she oversees.

Fenodyree

Traditionally a faerie spirit from the Isle of Man, a Fenodyree (sometimes
spelled phynodderee, phynnodderee, fynnoderee, or fenoderee) is a small
hairy man, often called a sprite or faun-like being. Like the Scottish brownies, he is often a helpful friendly spirit, and if willing, is known in folklore to
help with tasks requiring great strength or endurance such as carrying rocks

---

9. Margaret Ann Courtney, *Cornish Feasts and Folk-Lore* (AlbaCraft Publishing. 1886. Kindle
   Edition), 70.

long distances or mowing an entire field. He is sometimes called *yn foldyr gastey—the nimble mower,* for this reason. The Glashtin, known only in the southern Isle of Man, may be the same kind of faery spirit as the Fenodyree.

The Brownie and the Brùnaidh

Brownies are usually friendly household spirits who care for the house and lands around it, and are famous especially for their farm work. Farmsteads lucky enough to have a brownie would leave them offerings from the various produce the farm grew or made, and in return they would help with the brewing, milk churning, and the reaping and sowing of the crops. On a small now-uninhabited island called the Isle of Vallay near North Uist is a stone called the Brownie stone, which used to be given an offering of milk every Sunday.[10]

Like the Gruagach, the Brownie should never be given any clothes in thanks, as this causes great offence and will cause them to vanish and leave the house forever. Another name for the Brownie was the Brùnaidh, although this being was slightly different in that he was often known as a mischievous spirit who should not be thanked at all for his help but would still receive offerings of milk. The Brùnaidh insisted that all the doors be left open lest he cause great trouble, and cause the dogs to bark, or tip pails of water about the house. In some places, the dogs would need to be left outside at night or it was said the Brùnaidh would kill them, and he would violently attack those who made a mess in the house at night or approached it with ill intent.[11]

Brownies and Brùnaidh are later-day versions of the old household gods who were venerated at the hearthside or at a special altar or shrine. While these folktales usually involve examples from larger farms and even stately houses, every household will have its household spirits who are intimately connected to the land on which the house is built and have dwelt there long

10. Martin Martin, *A Description of the Western Islands of Scotland* (London: A. Bell, 1776), republished in Kindle edition (AlbaCraft Publishing, 2013), location 787.

11. John Gregorson Campbell, *Superstitions of the Highlands and Islands of Scotland* (Glasgow: James MacLehose and Sons. 1900) republished in Kindle (Albacraft Publishing 2012), 2117.

before the humans came. Befriending these spirits with offerings of milk or other dairy produce, and with acts of care for the home and surrounding land can help to build a deep and fruitful relationship with them. When considering spirits who appear to have some domestic role, its always useful to remember that the land and the spirits dwelling there have a history far older than any building; to bless or clear the energies in a home, one needs to primarily attend to the land itself.

Gruagach

Some tales in the Scottish Highlands describe the Gruagach as a hairy wild man who teaches skills with the sword or a long-haired warrior, but most tales describe them as a fair-haired fairy woman often wearing a conical hat. She oversees the cattle and cares for them casting her protective magic upon them. Gruagachs were usually given a libation of milk poured over special *clach na gruagaich* or Gruagach stones. These were usually low, flat-topped stones often described these days as *glacial erratics* that stand out from the local stones in an area often due to their different geology and unusual placements. Many Gruagach stones have a slight dip or naturally formed bowl like cavity upon them which was used for the offering. Such stones have been found throughout Scotland and the Hebrides as far as Arran, Islay, Mull, Tiree, Iona, Harris, Lewis, Cawdor, Culloden, and Lochaber, and a special rhyme was sung or intoned when the offering was made.

'A ghruagach, a ghruagach,
Cum suas mo spreidhe,
Cum sios an Guaigean,
Cum uap an Geige.
Brownie, brownie,
Uphold my herds,
Keep down the'Guaigean,
Keep from them the Geige.[12]

---

12. Alexander Carmichael, *Carmina Gadelica Vol. II* (Edinburgh: T. and A. Constable, 1900), 306.
   http://www.sacred-texts.com/neu/celt/cg2/cg2111.htm.

(Note: The Guaigen and the Geige are spirits connected to death or bringing death to those they touch.)

Traditional Tales

The Gruagach of East Bennan (Scottish)

The Gruagach lived at East Bennan in a cave which is still called 'uamh na gruagaich'—cave of the Gruagach, and "uamh na beiste"—cave of the monster. She herded the cattle of the townland of Bennan, and no spring-loss, no death-loss, no mishap, no murrain, ever befell them, while they throve and fattened and multiplied right well.

The Gruagach would come forth with the radiant sun, her golden hair streaming on the morning breeze, and her rich voice filling the air with melody. She would wait on a grassy hillock afar off till the people would bring out their 'creat-airean,' creatures, crooning a lullaby the while, and striding to and fro. The following is a fragment of one of her songs:

Ho, hi, ho! mach na boidhean,
Boidhean boidheach brogach beannach,
Ho, hi, ho! mach na boidhean.
Crodh Mhicugain, crodh Mhiceannain,
Crodh MhicFhearachair mhoir a Bheannain,
Ho, hi, ho! mach na boidhean.
Corp us carn air graisg na Beurla,
Mharbh iad orm mo cheile falaich,
Ho, hi, ho! mach na boidhean.
Ruisg iad mi gu ruig mo leine,
Struill agus streuill mo leannan,
Ho, hi, ho! mach na boidhean.
Oidhch an Arainn, oidhch an Ile,
'S an Cinntire uaine a bharraich,
Ho, hi, ho! mach na boidhean.'

Ho, hi, ho! out the kine,[13]
Pretty cattle hoofed and horned,
Ho, hi, ho! out the kine.
Cows of MacCugan, cows of Mackinnon,
Cows of big Macfarquhar of the Bennan,
Ho, hi, ho! out the kine.
Corpse and cairn to the rabble English,
They have killed my hidden lover,
Ho, hi, ho! out the kine.
They have stripped me to my shift,
They have clubbed and torn my lover,
Ho, hi, ho! out the kine.
A night in Arran, a night in Islay,
And in green Kintyre[14] of birches,
Ho, hi, ho! out the kine.

The people of Bennan were so pleased with the tender care the Gruagach took of their corn and cattle that they resolved to give her a linen garment to clothe her body and down sandals to cover her feet. They placed these on a knoll near the Gruagach and watched from afar. But instead of being grateful she was offended, and resented their intrusion so much that she determined to leave the district. She placed her left foot on Ben Bhuidhe in Arran and her right foot on Allasan, Ailsa Craig, making this her stepping-stone to cross to the mainland of Scotland or to Ireland. While the Gruagach was in the act of moving her left foot, a three-masted ship passed beneath, the mainmast of which struck her in the thigh and overturned her into the sea. The people of Bennan

---

13. Kine—cattle.

14. Bennan is on the west coast of Scotland. Arran and Islay (pronounced *isla*) are both islands in the Hebrides, and Kintyre is a south western Scottish peninsula; all these destinations are relatively close to one another.

mourned the Gruagach long and loudly, and bewailed their own officiousness.[15]

☽ PRACTICAL ☾
SEEKING A FAERY FRIEND

Gaining allies known as the *Co-Choisiche* or the *Coimimeadh* (Scots Gaelic, "the one who steps with you," or "co-traveller") and other spirit contacts when working with faery and and the otherworld is very important. The spirit world in its various forms is neither positive or negative but instead functions as a great cauldron that transforms and evolves; it is the deep energies in the earth, the earth's very soul; here, you can interact with the consciousness of those who dwell on the surface realms of the material plane. It can be an excellent place for healing and learning about yourself in a deeper way, but it is easy to get lost in the endless reflections of our awareness that we may find there without a guide or friend. Equally, not all spirits and faery beings we may encounter are friendly: some may have no interest in us, and others may have harmful intentions for a whole variety of reasons. Humanity has not always been good to the earth or respectful of spirit; while some spirit beings may have a malignant nature, it's more common to find beings who are resentful, wary, or in need of healing or a sign that we intend to honour and restore between us all the sacred bonds that once existed (and still do, in many ways). Though it is important to be cautious, the Celtic otherworld is not a place to fear—it is, however, a place to respect and bring our self-knowledge as well as the vital knowledge that what we encounter there are spirit beings in their own right, not merely aspects of ourselves. Not everything exists to serve or help us. So, we must be like independent travellers who learn the terrain (and the language, if we can), seek a guide, and keep our eyes open.

Try the following exercise to connect with the faery realms of the Celtic otherworld and seek an ally or faery friend to assist you.

---

15. Carmichael, *Carmina Gadelica Vol. II*, 308.

Sitting comfortably, preferably out in nature somewhere where you will not be disturbed or in some sacred space indoors, settle yourself and take three deep slow breaths. Try to sit with your back straight, either cross-legged or with your bare feet flat on the ground. Really tune into the earth beneath you. Remember that you are ultimately part of one planet-sized ecosystem and organism, and breathe slowly with the earth, letting Her hold you and support your body. After a while, begin to breathe that connection with the earth into your body—see it in your inner vision as life-giving sap, or golden-green light. Let it slowly fill your body and your energy field, your soul or aura. Give it plenty of time.

With your inner vision, imagine an archway of two oak trees before you with a pale stone path leading through a forest ahead of you. This forest is a vast and timeless place, the great boreal forest of spirit that spans all times and across all the northern lands from Siberia to Scotland to Canada to Mongolia. All things may be found here, for the forest is rich in secrets and wonders. First gaze along the path ahead of you; in your mind, set your intention to seek a faery ally. Say out loud to the woods ahead of you: "I come in friendship and respect to seek a guide to the faery realms and an ally in this place!" Use your own words as you wish. See your bare feet on the path and begin to walk along it through the trees. Take note of the feel of the air and the light—is it day or night? Dawn or dusk? Let the vision before you grow in depth and detail. As you follow the path, you are gradually led up a wide hillside through the trees. The path turns and arcs ahead of you, and you sense you may be ascending a hill by a spiralling way. Up and up and round and round. You hear the sound of hooves upon the path and see a flash of white ahead. For a moment, you see the slender form of a white deer leaping and running ahead of you in the distance. Was it a stag or a hind?

You begin to sense a change in the atmosphere and from time to time almost hear music in the distance that seems to vanish as soon as you pay attention. You continue on your way until you see a large earthen mound rise up before you through the trees. Whether it is day or night, the mound seems to shine with its own special light, quite different from the surrounding area.

As you approach the mound, you see a figure sitting quietly by the trees. Will this be your ally? How does your heart feel? Your gut? You may approach the figure, or they may come to you. Tell them you come in friendship and with respect, seeking an ally. How do they respond?

Finding your ally may be simple and successful on your first visit, or you may need to return to this place over and over until you find the right guide for you whom you can call for inner vision work, as you walk upon the land, or with any other activity. A faery ally is a great thing and must be treasured, but it cannot be forced. Good luck and blessings upon your seeking!

If the being before you is your ally, you will find the connection and conversation is clear and forms well. However, you are under no obligation to accept an ally who doesn't feel right to you. If things do feel right on this occasion, ask a little about how to learn about faery and the otherworld, as well as how to build your connection with your ally. However, if too many questions don't feel right, do not rush; trust the process that a good start has been made and return another time. After a while, it will be time to return along the path through the forest. Thank your ally, and return to your body, repeating the route in reverse, not deviating off the path.

Take some deep breaths feeling the air in your lungs and the blood in your veins. Open your eyes and wiggle your fingers and toes to feel fully back to your body.

The Fetch or Co-walker

The fetch, sometimes known as the *Taise* (Irish) or the *Coimimeadh* (Scots Gaelic meaning "co-traveller" or "co-walker") is an ally who has always been with you throughout your life, though you may not know it. Having a conscious and clear relationship with your fetch is deeply personal and powerful and marks a certain level of self-knowledge and psychic clarity. Much like the co-walkers or *Coimimeadh* described by the Rev. Robert Kirk in his excellent treatise on the Scottish Faery faith, *The Secret Commonwealth of Elves, Fauns and Faeries*, the fetch may take on any form and shift and change forms at will. Often a faery of some kind, the fetch is your lifelong spirit ally who experiences some measure of the mortal world by literally walking with you in life. In exchange, they may help you with deeper or long-term patterns and spiritual growth. A fetch or co-walker can be a really useful ally. Their presence can be strongly felt, or they can simply give you a subtle sense that you are accompanied in some way at certain points in your life, depending on the relationship you build with them. There is no fixed tradition on how these allies will work with you as everyone is different, but working with a fetch can be powerful magic and affect real change. Working together can also help the practitioner with life-long challenges and even broader soul evolution.

In Irish folklore, the fetch is said to have the exact appearance of the person it accompanies; when seen (often at a distance by someone who knows the person is in fact somewhere else miles away), it is said to be an omen of their death. However, there are far more firsthand accounts of a fetch being seen where this is not the outcome, and I have seen numerous fetches over the years, none of which foretold a death. Instead, a fetch may go somewhere ahead of the person it accompanies to check out the area beforehand, bring something back from there, or alert whoever spots them that the person they resemble is in need of assistance or will be visiting soon.

❱ PRACTICAL ❰
CALLING IN THE FETCH

We've all had those times where we feel like someone is right beside or behind us. This presence is often your fetch, although that's not the only interpretation. At other times, a fetch may come to you in dreams or you may repeatedly see an image in your daily life that invokes a deeper emotional stirring and evokes their presence. A relationship with a fetch is something people often become aware of as they grow older; the many times they have either felt their presence or dreamt of them becomes understood as a pattern that takes form over many years. The fetch is the main spirit who can help you regain lost instincts and intuitions not just for yourself but your whole bloodline. With them, you can heal long-standing patterns that persist through generations, as the fetch may have helped your ancestors before you. By forming a close relationship with this spirit, you may find your wild inner self returning to help you walk through life with a sense of balance and inner connection previously thought impossible.

Calling in your fetch takes time, and the effort is best made with your heart as the main leader and teacher. Make offerings to the fetch; perhaps set aside a special place in your home where you leave offerings and also place things that help invoke the deeper feeling which comes with its presence. As you find times in your day when you are alone, speak to it as you would a life-long friend, and look out for the subtle touch of its presence. Keep a dream journal and record your dreams with the sense that it has perhaps taken many forms over time but with the same feeling in every instance. Court it as a lover or your own soul—after all, it carries with it your deepest desires, plans, and knowledge from one life to another. Treat it with patience and courtesy, asking that it becomes known to you, and treat it with honour and care. In time, it will show itself to you more and more, and you may be able to access its wisdom with greater ease and clarity. There is no map for this practice, as it is the deepest magical relationship and you must bring your most authentic self to the task, without preconceived ideas or projections.

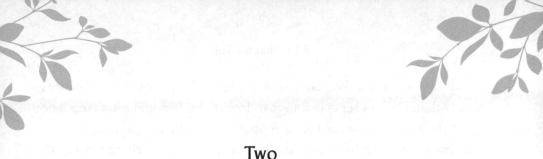

Two

EARTH

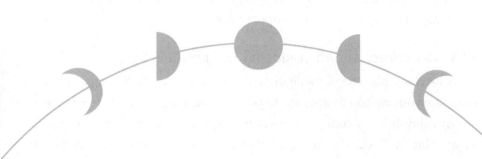

In the Celtic traditions, the triplicity of earth, sea, and sky or air as three realms (with the fourth element of fire held as sacred but separate) repeats itself often in the surviving lore. For this reason we will explore the traditions of each realm and element separately, beginning first with the element and realm of the earth, of manifestation and material life as well as rock and soil and planet earth herself.

Earth Magic, Earth Awareness

The earth has been the repository for so much negativity in these last few centuries, with all the environmental damage and disrespect it endures. It has been seen as dirty, crude, and something a spiritual seeker needs to ascend away from or escape. This viewpoint justifies so much horror and damage. Once, nations around the world honoured the earth as goddess, giver of life, the source of all things, the seat of wisdom and beneficence, but no longer. She has become in humanity's eyes a resource to be abused for short-term gain. By returning to this vision of her inner spirit, her ever-present and embodied deity, we can shift a great deal of that ignorance into awareness again. We can make changes at the roots of our connection with her from user and abuser to loving children and caretakers once again. Should we honour her, a fundamental shift in our consciousness may result, one which can fuel and inspire our ability to change our material lives and find solutions large and small to correct the damage. We can heal the wounds we have inflicted. The focus here is not guilt or shame but power and responsibility—every day, every generation has the chance to change. This is our turn, our opportunity.

Ways to Connect with the Land and Its Indwelling Soul

Walk barefoot, plant trees, meditate while sitting on the earth, create land art, calculate your carbon footprint and take practical regular steps to reduce it. Clean rubbish from your area. Switch to green electricity or solar panels in your home. Reduce your car journeys. Reduce or eliminate your plastic use. Grow your own food. Buy local. Recycle. Recycle. Recycle. Honour the living earth and all biodiversity.

◗ PRACTICAL ◖
BUILDING RELATIONSHIPS

In general, a relationship with the earth means really getting to know your landscape and spending as much time in nature as you can, even if that means getting out into a park or small local woodland. Most cities have some green spaces that can be explored to the full. The land spirits in built up areas often respond well to signs of care and connection. What's even better is spending time in more remote, wild places. Connection with the land takes time; earth spirits are not to be rushed, and patience is needed. Really take time, learning about the land around you, its flora and fauna, how rivers and springs travel across the land if any, how it changes through the seasons and its patterns of growth and decline, how it responds to different weather and of course, how different areas on the landscape feel. Allow each part of the land around you to show you its unique character, its energy and presence.

After a while, areas on the landscape that have a more magical or spirit-dwelling feeling will gradually become apparent. Look for places near water, or entrances to the earth, but equally look out for places with a special beauty or quality to the light. It may be somewhere that just feels nice or equally somewhere with a special tree or marvellous view … sometimes it is a place where the play of light and shade creates a beautiful effect, or somewhere a stream sings an especially lovely song as you pass, or the place where you notice the birds roost or sing at dusk. Let your subtle inner senses and a feeling for beauty reveal a place to you. Equally look out for places which feel more gloomy or sad. These may be places that need your care. Every landscape is different, and taking the time to get to know them as you would a group of friends takes time and sensitivity. Do not project too many of your own ideas upon the land, even if it has interesting or famous folklore. Allow its unique nature to speak to you in its own way. You may well find the legends and stories about a place ring true when you get to know it well, but do not come to it with your preconceived ideas; let it reveal itself to you over time, if it chooses to.

If you begin to feel as though you have found an area with a special feeling or magic, pay extra attention to it, and spend more time there. When you first go, don't bring an agenda—just visit regularly, and give it your time and patience. Learn to notice its details.

After a while you may decide to bring the place offerings—a little gift of song, or a little cream poured at the base of a tree perhaps. Make sure whatever you offer is biodegradable and does no harm. A gift of bird food is good, or you can spend time cleaning away rubbish every time you pass. Give the land your time—the spirits always notice such things.

Eventually when the time feels right, see if you are able to connect with its indwelling spirit, its genius loci, or another guardian caretaking being. Find a place to sit comfortably. Really slow yourself down, quiet your mind, and breathe slowly and deeply. Feel the earth beneath you and the sky above.

Try to notice as you breathe the smells around you, the scent of the earth, the water, the trees—are they in leaf or wintery twigs? How does the wind move sitting here, does it reach you or is the place closed off and screened by plants or geographical features like a hill, or a bank? What is it like to sit here?

Now gently try to stretch your awareness out from yourself, and let yourself acknowledge the spirit presences around you—you may not feel them overtly, but let yourself accept that they are present.

Close your eyes, and breathe slow and deep, maintaining that feeling of being fully present as much as you can, and ask them to come and reveal themselves to you. State that you come in friendship and respect, and to learn from them what the land is like from their perspective. Communicate with them honestly, and simply, and wait for a response. It's always best to use your own words, but try this as an example:

"Guardian spirits of this place, I come in friendship, may you show yourself to me, so I may learn your ways?"

Keep breathing slow and deep. Keep that sense of inner balance and presence. Let your senses stretch out around you. You may feel a presence around or behind you, you may feel a breath of wind upon your cheek or notice that a leaf has fluttered into your lap. Equally you may have a clear sense of a being ready to communicate with you in words or other gestures. Be open to all possibilities; allow everything you experience to be a form of communication for you to interpret with your inner knowing, your heart or your belly rather than your mind.

Allow the experience to be just as it is. Thank the spirits clearly. Leave them an offering again or show some other form of care for the place. Repeat the exercise when you return again. This technique evolves and grows like the land itself. It takes time, but eventually it will blossom into a clear sense of relationship, a two-way avenue of communication and communion.

Hag Stones

Hag stones are pebbles or lumps of stone with naturally occurring holes in them that go all the way through. These are powerful and ancient charms for protection that also assist in seeing spirits and faeries of all kinds. Hag stones function as doorways to other realms when held up to the eye and looked through. Used in this manner, a hag stone allows the practitioner to see things usually unseen. Spirits of all kinds may be discerned, as can energetic injuries and other phenomena such as elf-shot—when someone's energy field or physical body has been injured by a spirit weapon or elf arrows. The spirit of the hag stone itself should always be honoured as an earth spirit in its own right and remembered as a friend. To own a hag stone is a powerful blessing. Strung up by the door with red thread, it is a powerful guardian that shall let no ill will cross the threshold.

Reading the Wild

Really feeling in tune with the nature around you can take time and practice, and good observation. Learning about all the animals and plants that frequent the land around you can take time, but opens up another world of interconnectedness that is a spiritual and magical practice in its own right, enmeshing your spiritual life into the everyday world around you. In this way, the world itself may become your divination tool, you may find you can navigate your day on the clues and directions the greater web of life reveals to you.

☽ PRACTICAL ☾
NATURE AWARENESS

Sit out in a spot in nature and try just being there in silence for twenty minutes. Take that time to be still and notice every living thing around you—every plant and tree, every animal and insect. Repeat this once a week or once a day (if you can), and repeat the exercise throughout a whole season, or even better, a whole year. The longer you sit in stillness and quiet, the more animals and birds will begin to relax and reveal themselves. Gradually you will notice the shifts and changes, and the things which remain unchanged. Certain features will show themselves as central points in an area, ecologically or energetically, and others will gain a prominence for a certain period of time. For example, you will notice certain birds will love a certain tree, while in another a particular insect will swarm, but just for the season. Try this at dawn and dusk, and notice the change between the creatures of the day and the creatures of the night.

I try to engage with this practice every day if I can and have been blessed to have seen an entire herd of wild deer come past me, feeding calmly while I sat in silence. British wildlife is very nervous as we don't have many vast wild spaces, but I have sat while badgers snuffled and played at my feet. I have a favourite place to sit by an old oak tree where owls nest and watched them come home and go out hunting without any disturbance, close enough to touch. Owls, for example, are powerful spirit allies and connecting with them in this way creates a bond that will help serve us well in daily life as well as in spiritual work; they also remind us that we are living in a won-derful world full of its own living magic. Sitting quietly reduces much of the alarm an animal will feel at your coming into an area, and it is amazing what you will see. Over time, you will notice the differences and locations of birdsong, nests and burrows, small rodents scurrying home with food, and larger beasts such as deer, which are often able to go unseen despite their size. You'll also notice which birds will tolerate each other and which won't, and even how an area changes when people or a predator arrives or leaves. You'll also begin to notice a whole host of other details your land uniquely contains, which you would otherwise miss. Given time, you will find that you can often recognise a type of tree by the sound the wind makes in its leaves before seeing it (which will change by season). You will also eventually know the best places to forage any needed plant materials at any time of the year—not merely their location but which conditions and areas grow the best specimens with the greatest lifeforce and fecundity. You will regain your own wild knowledge of an area, your own animal senses and instincts, your own place in the subtle and magical weaving of the land.

☽ PRACTICAL ☾
WISDOM FROM THE EARTH

When you feel you know your landscape really well, it's possible to open yourself up into continuous communication with it and let nature and your place among and within it inform you of changes in energy and atmosphere, and even illuminate you with regards to issues in your own life. We and nature are in constant relation, immersed in one another whether we are aware of it or not. This infinite web of connection performs very well as a living divination system if we are sensitive and present enough to heed the signs.

) PRACTICAL (
FEELING THE WEB

The next time you are out in nature, set out upon a walking mediation to simply become more aware of your surroundings and more attuned to the subtle communications and interrelations between all things.

Begin by just breathing. Imagine in your inner vision the vast, infinite web that connects you to all of creation, and all that is not creation—all of space and time. See yourself as a single point and moment within it. Don't give this part too much time if this doesn't suit you; just imagine that you are connected to everything around you, near and far, and that you are both a point within the web and also are traveling along a single thread.

As you take your walk, be quietly aware of the background of this web and the thread that you are travelling along and aim to become gently more and more aware of your feet upon the earth and your place of exact presence upon the earth—this spot, here, where you stand.

As you walk, allow your awareness to gently move out beyond you, and let all of nature around you in turn be a communication, and an expression, of *All* of the web. Be aware of sensations in your body, of your solar plexus, and your heart especially. As you move, notice the shifts in your own mood, and the atmosphere of the places you walk, the subtle changes of light and temperature, as well as the presence of natural features, rocks and trees for example, the behaviour of animals and the flight of birds, as well as any energetic, spiritual sensations you feel. Have no agenda, just open awareness of your place upon the web and the experience of witnessing the expression of creation around you. Notice the voice of nature in all its forms and everything else that comes up as you walk. Don't analyse, just witness—be peaceful and receptive.

Take as many walks in this way as you can, and you will gradually become aware of animals and different types of trees and plants you never noticed at first, as well as energetic spaces and spirit presences, threads and paths of energy more distinct than others, some far finer and more subtle.

This practice has much to teach about the difference between how spirit and magic are explained in the rational sense and what we are actually engaging with; what we truly *are* in relation to everything else. It can be very humbling but also incredibly empowering as you begin to learn the land, and it begins to learn about you. It is also very healing.

You may be surprised to note that the rhythm and mood of what you see in nature may be mirrored in what happens to the lives of people in your area on that day. After a while, you may notice the interrelation between things—the flight of birds over a river as bad weather approaches, the roiling dance of autumn leaves down the road in the flow of a gust of wind. These may become indicators and signs of the wider energetic landscape, ways to divine wider events as well as your personal matters. It takes time, but tune in to read and take heed of the signs. This is an organic art more than a linear, logical thing to learn, but you'll train yourself into that instinctual knowing that our ancient ancestors and animal cousins take for granted.

☽ PRACTICAL ☾
READING THE WEB

Let's say you have an important meeting (business or personal) or something that could do with some inner preparation. On the day of the meeting, what is the first thing you see and hear when you first awake? Take note of simple details, as these are the first tracks as it were, upon the web you will be travelling along through life on that day. Just before you leave, imagine setting forth upon an infinite web of information and connection between you and all things. Remember that all things and infinite possibilities surround us at all times with every opportunity to redirect our course whenever we choose. Ask your spirit allies now to guide you to the best result of your meeting—be as clear as possible about defining the destination you choose for the outcome of your day. Take three deep breaths to be centred and really present. Be clear with your intention as you leave the house. What are the first noises you hear outside? What are the first things you see as you step outside? Don't worry if you live in an urban or city environment, it's the same. As you travel, do so in a relaxed way. Take heed of signs on buses, house names, road signs, as well as more natural things such as trees by the roadside or the flight of birds. Don't dismiss the flight of the pigeon or the seagull, the child who crosses your path or the old woman sitting on the bench. Allow them to form a narrative in your mind, each a symbol of the process you are engaging in.

As you approach your destination, become aware of entering an energetic bubble that is the environment for your meeting—this can be large, across many streets, or the size of the room. How do you feel as you come to this new threshold? Give yourself time to breathe and become centred, holding this new information as the advice from a friend.

☾ PRACTICAL ☽
A NATURAL DIVINATION KIT

Intimate knowledge of your landscape can be helpful in many ways; a closer relationship to the land means a closer relationship to the spirits, whether you are able to work with them clearly, or feel a need for tools to assist you. One such useful tool is a natural divination kit made of found objects. Often, this is a collection of something like thirteen to thirty small, natural (or mainly natural) found objects. It's fine to include some man-made objects, so long as they feel right to you. Those who live in cities may perhaps add small items found in shops and markets to this, but the point isn't to buy things—it's to gradually attain a set of small useable items that express the landscape and all its inhabitants to you. This kit works in many ways, so how you make it depends on your landscape, feelings, preferences, and personal path. Each item needs to come to you or be found by you, and it works best if you acknowledge the indwelling spirit in each thing you find and take time to become aware of any symbolic meanings and let ideas about usage come to you. Creating your own divination set can take time—in fact it's best of you don't rush, but take time to let the kit build, even over many years, adding things and occasionally letting things go according to their own direction or instruction.

You will need a simple cloth or leather bag to store your items in, as well as a casting cloth (optional), a square of material to cast your items upon.

You may also want to include a diary or notebook to record any observations and readings performed with your kit so that you may increase your knowledge as you become familiar with the kit.

Start by going to your sacred space—an altar in your home or a favourite place in nature. Ask the spirits of the land to grant you things you can use for guidance and divination. Some of these objects may become useful in spell work as well. Then go on a walk with the clear intention of finding your first item for your set. Take your time—after all, nature doesn't rush. Try to be as mindful and aware as you can as you walk through the woods or local park. Let something come to you. It may be a small pebble you find on your path, a feather, or some other small item. When you come across something, hold it in your hand and breathe with it for a while. Ask yourself, "Is this the item I am guided to?" If you feel the answer is yes, take some time to meditate with the object or perhaps perform a shamanic or visionary journey to seek communion with its spirit and divine its message to you.

Take care to thank the spirits and the object verbally each time you add something to your set, and don't try to get a complete set all at once. Let your collection build slowly, no more than one object at a time. Allow the area's energy and makeup to talk to you through what you find, no matter if they are silver coins, safety pins, oak galls, or balls of moss. Let the land have its voice and strive to create a set that helps you hear it.

Divining Interpretation

Allow each object to speak to you and take time to let yourself feel it. Your intuition will guide you here. Some things will have very specific energies and feelings attached to them, while other things may have more symbolic relevance, which is fine too.

Here's a list of common symbols for a natural divination set:

- Feather
- Round pebble
- Coin

- Heart shaped stone
- Acorn
- Oak gall
- Hazelnut
- Seashell
- Interesting twig
- Water polished glass
- Conker
- Red leaf
- Burnt stick
- Driftwood
- Tiny charm bottle of water
- Moss
- Animal tooth
- Claw
- Small bone
- Seed pod
- Ash keys
- Safety pin
- Crystal
- Rusty nail (blunt)

Using your set

You can use your set as soon as you have more than one thing in your bag. The easiest way to use it is to settle yourself, ask it a question, and dip your hand in to pull out the object that represents your answer. However, a more nuanced reading can be performed using techniques from other divination systems such as tarot.

Try a three-object reading for a simple past, present, and future answer or a twelve-object reading to represent the astrological houses for something more complex. These "spreads" can be laid upon your cloth, and you can go through them one object at a time to discern meaning in position and how they relate to one another.

One of the most interesting ways to use such a set is to perform a free-form divination also known as open casting: simply hold the bag, ask your question, and then reach in, grab a handful, and throw the objects gently upon the cloth. This technique requires good inner vision and sensitivity to work best but anyone can do it and it does get easier with practice. Take a few breaths and let your eyes rest upon the cloth and the objects. Consider them both individually and as a whole. What shapes do they make upon the cloth? Look out for a larger overall shape as well as "constellations" of smaller groups and patterns. Open up your senses and ignore your more logical thinking—allow yourself to feel what the objects are saying. Trust yourself and your relationship with the objects to reveal the meaning.

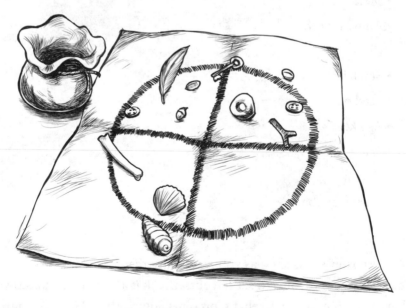

Natural Divination Kit

Some people like to overlay a pattern in the mind's eye over their open cast readings, such as the wheel of the year or the zodiac and see these positions as well as the items to guide their interpretation, while others will use only their inner eye. Everyone is slightly different with these techniques, so it is best to allow yourself to feel out how you do it.

All really good divination is a felt art rather than a logical, learnt thing. Although learning systems and symbols can help, it can only take you so far, so allow yourself to experiment and have fun, seeking out your own inner guidance to find a way that has meaning and power for you.

Animal Spirits and Guides

The Iron Age Celts had a powerful relationship with animals and animal spirits, working with them for magic and power, as well as for farming and hunting. The earliest hunter gatherers probably learnt a great deal from observing animals in the wild and these traits continued to be observed and utilised to build a whole body of lore relating to animal spirits and allies as well as practical uses, which survived into the modern era, becoming the animal lore of the later sixteenth to nineteenth centuries. This animal knowledge is being revived today, and there are great projects throughout Britain and Ireland to restore land for wildlife and even reintroduce animals which became extinct in the British landscape over the last few hundred years such as boars, beavers, and white-tailed sea eagles.

Cernunnos and the Wild Herdsman

Iron age Celts everywhere, but most notably in Gaul, venerated a horned deity who was associated with antlers, deer, serpents, and other animals. This figure is commonly called Cernunnos, most likely from the Celtic word *cer*, meaning *horn*. Epigraphic evidence for his worship is found on the famous "Pillar of the boatmen" found in Paris, original home of the Parisii tribe dating to about 14 CE, as well as in Luxembourg where a metal plaque dedicated to him was found, probably made by the local Treveri tribe. Arguments have been made that associate Cernunnos with the medieval English figure Herne and the eighth-century CE Irish figure Conall Cernach, found in the *Táin Bó Fraích* (cattle raid on Fraech) of the Ulster cycle. Other horned gods are found throughout the Celtic diaspora; petroglyphs and sculptures of horned gods have been found in Cisalpine

Gaul and Celtiberia. The most famous Cernunnos figure is found in relief on the Gundestrup Cauldron, found in Jutland in 1891. Arguments for dating this are complex and vary from around 150 to 100 BCE; other, wilder arguments date it to anywhere up to 300 CE, but these are less convincing. The Cernunnos relief on the cauldron gives us his most classic appearance, suited, sitting cross legged, with antlers and torcs, holding a horned serpent. Here we see him as a shamanic, meditative figure, lord of the animals, but posed as still, connected, rather than hunting or herding… giving us great clues into how to use this ancestral path to connect with spirits and with the land around us, and how to work with Cernunnos himself.

☽ PRACTICAL ☾
CERNUNNOS—SEEKING WISDOM
FROM THE WILD HUNTSMAN

Try this exercise to connect with the wild huntsman and deepen your connection with the animal spirits.

Find a place to sit comfortably, preferably in nature somewhere where you will not be disturbed, or equally in some sacred space indoors if need be. Settle yourself and take three deep, slow breaths. Try to sit with your back straight and either cross legged or with your bare feet flat on the ground. Really tune into the earth beneath you, remember you are ultimately part of one planet sized ecosystem and organism, and breath slowly with the earth, letting Her hold you and support your body. After a while, begin to breathe that connection with the earth into your body, see it in your inner vision as life giving sap, or golden green light, and let it slowly fill your body and your energy field, your soul or aura. Give it plenty of time.

In your inner vision, gradually imagine an archway of two oak trees before you with a path of pale stone leading through a forest. This forest is a vast and timeless place—it is the great boreal forest of spirit that spans all times across all the northern lands from Siberia to Scotland to Canada to Mongolia. All things may be found here, for the forest is rich in secrets and wonders. See your bare feet on the path and walk along it through the trees.

Take note of the feel of the air and light—is it day or night? Dawn or dusk? Let the vision before you grow in depth and detail. What trees can you see? What animals? How does it feel to enter this great and ancient place?

In time, the path leads you to a large, sacred clearing. The Celts called them *Nemetons*, or sacred groves, and in the centre of the clearing is a great tall oak tree, ancient and resplendent. This is known in Ireland as the *Bile*, the sacred world tree where gods and men gather. As soon as you enter this sacred enclosure, you notice a shift in the atmosphere—a stillness, a sense of power in the air. Take your time and wander around the space, feeling yourself present in this place between the worlds.

In time you notice the birdsong and hear beneath it a slow, quiet music—it is the sound of flutes and the wind in the reeds, thrumming and soaring among the birdsong. The melody seems to weave in and out of your perception before growing stronger and clearer. Shapes begin to emerge from the trees, and you find yourself in a gathering of many beings—men, women, birds, animals of every kind—assemble before the oak and sit quietly before it. You take your place among them.

The tree before you is enormous, far bigger than any tree you have seen before; it is like a giant sentient being, aware and thrumming with vitality and power. For a while you are dazzled by its sheer presence, but after a while you begin to see a figure sitting at its base among its roots. The figure is a man, several times larger than any living man with great antlers springing from his brow. His eyes are deep and dark as a forest pool, and you notice a great serpent coiled at his feet. It rears its head to him as he sits in contemplation.

Spend some time with this ancient god of the greenwood; seek his wisdom. You may ask questions or be shown mysteries. Consider here your relationship with nature, the forest itself, and with all wild places. Consider your relationship with the animal kingdom. What can you do to strengthen your bonds with the wild world?

When you feel it is time or he dismisses you, thank Cernunnos. Turning your back, return the way you came along the path.

Cernunnos

Take some deep breaths; feel the air in your lungs and the blood in your veins. Open your eyes and wiggle your fingers and toes to feel fully back to your body.

☽ PRACTICAL ☾
ANIMAL ALLIES

Take practical steps in the real world to support ecology and especially animal welfare. Increase your knowledge of the animals that live around you—there are a great may animal species living wild even in cities. What can you do to support them and build your connection with the animal world? What environmental lifestyle and consumerist changes can you make? Are there places you can give your money and/or time to support the animals of the world?

❯ PRACTICAL ❨
SEEKING ANIMALS IN THE WILD

Note: What follows is no substitute for common sense and should not be used to approach dangerous animals, to aid hunting, or to put yourself at risk in any way. If you are tracking an animal that may be dangerous, avoid it. Take time to learn about the animal's specific behaviours before trying this exercise, and always take responsibility for your safety.

A technique long used by hunters and shamans in many parts of the world is to mimic an animal's behaviour. For instance, early humans may have learned to hunt by copying wolves, and many shamanic cultures have ceremonies where the spirits of animals are invoked and copied in their stances and movements in order to draw in their wisdom and power. One technique used when stalking deer is to slowly dip your head and torso down straight while keeping your eyes locked on the animal; another that can work with birds is to tip or angle the head to mimic the head movements. At other times, going to a place where you can watch animals unobserved can be an amazing experience, but you must have great patience and forethought. The most common method is to construct an animal hideout of branches and leaves or use a camouflaged tent.

Tracking and stalking animals takes a lot of knowledge and experience, but the goal doesn't have to be hunting—you can instead use these methods to gain a deeper knowledge of an animal and walk in closer connection to the wild environment, holding a quieter and more humble presence in the forest or any natural environment. This technique can be used with no animal in mind but will transform your experience of walking through nature and maximise the chances of coming across animals unawares.

Start with both feet on the ground, standing calm and relaxed. Somehow animals see you easier if your body language is tense.

Slowly raise one of your feet and stand with all of your body weight on the opposite leg, balancing like a heron. Be fully conscious about where you will put your foot down. Gently place your foot down so as it will cause no noise, smoothly shifting your balance. If it causes sound, go very slowly. If you feel unbalanced, back off onto the other foot again and adjust. Repeat with the other foot, going slowly and being fully present in your surroundings and the placement of both feet. Your stride will be shorter and slower, but with practice, it can feel very relaxed and fluid. Breathe slowly, drop your shoulders, feel yourself in contact with the earth, all your tension sinking downwards, softly. With practice you can become very quiet indeed, and leave minimal tracks yourself.

If you can see an animal, allow your movements to reflect what is happening. If the animal is alert and looking around or listening, still yourself calmly and wait. Let yourself be aware but peaceful; let your consciousness melt into the trees and nature around you, and you will draw less attention. Wait until it goes back to feeding and starts making a bit of noise.

If it is relatively safe, go barefoot or use soft footwear rather than thick boots so you can feel the contours of the ground.

Try to let your senses widen and your vision soften; take in peripheral details while focusing on your immediate steps or the animal you are watching. Be quiet and soft in your manner so that you can hear more around you and locate noises more effectively.

Note which way the wind is blowing. Stay downwind of the animal you are watching so it doesn't smell you.

Pay attention. Be still when the air is still, and take advantage of the wind blowing and the noises it brings to mask your movements. Rainfall noises are also helpful in this way. It's easier to get close to an animal that is feeding or otherwise distracted than one who is already aware of you.

Take advantage of visual cover, trees, landscape features and areas of shadow. You'll be seen far easier approaching in an open space. Think ahead about the landscape and plan your route beforehand where possible.

Sometimes total silence is the only option. Be prepared to move your body according to the needs of the situation; you may have to crouch or even crawl. You may also need to stand perfectly still for an uncomfortable amount of time … extreme patience is sometimes needed if you want to draw close to an animal.

Pay attention to the birds. If you disturb the birds, it is likely the deer will notice and run.

Use the animal's own movement to your advantage. If you notice the animal is coming in your direction, try to hide yourself and get into a good position beforehand.

Remember that you too are an animal; nearly all of your ancestors except those of the last century or two used these skills all the time. Work on staying centred and present. Let your shoulders drop and your intuition awaken. Your common sense will kick in if you are calmly aware of yourself and your position in the landscape. Let your inner animal and your inner hunter guide you. Your body knows the way.

Animal Familiars

An animal familiar or helping spirit is the perfect ally to help you navigate your ordinary day-to-day life and keep your awareness empowered and present for the gifts and challenges of the middle realm. Animal allies can be worked with in many ways. They can provide insight and comfort in troubling times as well as emotional support, psychic protection, and inspiration that helps you to adopt their unique characteristics for solving problems and uncovering new trackways to your goals. They can encourage resilience as well as improving your instincts and intuition.

❯ PRACTICAL ❰
SEEKING YOUR FAMILIAR

Try this exercise to connect with an animal spirit to be your familiar, a guide and ally in the middle realm, the mortal realm. It builds upon your work to journey and meet Cernunnos in the wild wood.

As with the exercise above, where we contacted Cernunnos, we begin by sitting comfortably, preferably out in nature somewhere where you will not be disturbed, but equally in some sacred space indoors if need be. Settle yourself and take three deep slow breaths. Try to sit with your back straight and either cross legged or with your bare feet flat on the ground. Really tune into the earth beneath you and remember that you are ultimately part of one planet-sized ecosystem and organism. Breathe slowly with the earth, letting her hold you and support your body. After a while, begin to breath in that connection with the earth into your body; see it in your inner vision as life-giving sap or golden green light, and let it slowly fill your body and your energy field, your soul or aura. Give it plenty of time.

Just as we did before, gradually allow your inner vision to imagine an archway of the two oak trees before you with a pale stone path leading through the forest. Remember that this forest is a vast and timeless place, the great boreal forest of spirit that spans all times and across all the northern lands from Siberia to Scotland to Canada to Mongolia. All things may be found here, for the forest is rich in secrets and wonders. See your bare feet on the path and begin to walk along it through the trees. Take note of the feel of the air and the appearance of light—is it day or night? Dawn or dusk? Let the vision before you grow in depth and detail. What trees can you see? What animals? How does it feel to enter this great and ancient place?

In time, the path leads you to the large, sacred clearing. In the centre of the clearing is the great tall oak tree, ancient and resplendent. It is the Bile, the sacred world tree where gods and men gather. As soon as you enter this sacred enclosure, you notice a shift in the atmosphere ... a stillness, a sense of power in the air. Take your time to wander around the space and feel yourself present in this place between the worlds.

Eventually you notice birdsong and hear beneath it a slow quiet music, the sound of flute and the wind in reeds, thrumming and soaring among the birdsong. It seems to weave in and out of your perception before growing stronger and clearer. When you came here before, you encountered many beings and the great god Cernunnos himself. This time however, you wander the clearing alone and approach the great oak tree yourself. As you approach it, you reach out to touch its rough bark, and call out in your heart to meet your animal ally, your guide and animal kin.

A creature now emerges from the forest and approaches you in the centre of the clearing. It stands before you regarding you with bright, deep eyes. What animal is it? Does this feel right to you? You have permission to ask for another ally if this doesn't feel right—the world of the spirits has its own ways, and you may be tested or have many options. If you wish, return another time.

If you feel the animal in front of you is your ally, nod your head slowly, and look deep into its eyes. Ask it if it is willing to help you. It may respond with words or it may use body language or other signs and sounds. Spend time with your ally to ask it whatever questions you would like, bonding with it as you would a new friend.

When you feel it is time, ask your ally how it may work with you in the mortal world. After it responds, offer it your thanks and return the way you came along the path.

Take some deep breaths—feel the air in your lungs and the blood in your veins. Open your eyes and wiggle your fingers and toes to feel fully back to your body.

Fith-fath: Shapeshifting

Usually translated as "deer aspect," *fith-fath* is a Gaelic term referring to a charm and technique that may have its roots in hunting practices and is also described in numerous Celtic prayers, suggestive of earlier pre-Christian shapeshifting practices. Some of these verbal charms can be found in Scots Gaelic collections of prayers; an elemental version calling in the qualities of fire, lightning, sea, and earth can be found in *The Lorica of St Patrick*, a famous Irish protection prayer. Most call upon the spirit qualities of animals for magical power, protection and to invoke invisibility. A simple *fith-fath* can be found in the collection of lore from the Outer Hebrides, the *Carmina Gadelica*.

Fath fith

> Ni mi ort,
> Le Muire na frithe,
> Le Bride na brot,
> Bho chire, bho ruta,
> Bho mhise, bho bhoc,
> Bho shionn, 's bho mhac-tire,
> Bho chrain, 's bho thorc,

Bho chu, 's bho chat,
Bho mhaghan masaich,
Bho chu fasaich,
Bho scan foirir,
Bho bho, bho mharc,
Bho tharbh, bho earc,
Bho mhurn, bho mhac,
Bho iantaidh an adhar,

Fath fith
Will I make on thee,
By Mary of the augury,
By Bride of the corslet,
From sheep, from ram,
From goat, from buck,
From fox, from wolf,
From sow, from boar,
From dog, from cat,
From hipped-bear,
From wilderness-dog,
From watchful 'scan,'
From cow, from horse,
From bull, from heifer,
From daughter, from son.'[16]

Another, by the famous Scottish witch Isobel Gowdie, concerns turning into a hare:

I shall go into a hare,
With sorrow and sigh and mickle care;
And I shall go in the Devil's name
Ay till I come home again.'

---

16. Carmichael, *Carmina Gadelica Vol II*, 24–25.

To change back, the charm was:
'Hare, hare, God send thee care.
I am in a hare's likeness now,
But I shall be in a woman's likeness even now.[17]

☽ PRACTICAL ☾
SHAPESHIFTING

Do not try this exercise until you have fully recovered from any serious mental health issues and illnesses. Though shapeshifting can be very empowering, it requires a robust sense of self and a grounded attitude.

After you have completed the journey to meet your animal ally several times and feel you have established a good and trusting relationship with them, ask them to follow you back to the day-to-day middle world. When you have completed your inner journey, spend a few moments holding an awareness of your animal familiar with you and breathe with them in slow, deep breaths. Imagine in your inner vision that they are seated next to you and share your breathing. When you breathe out, they breathe in, when you breathe in, they breathe out. Do this for a few minutes before trying to move around, letting your movements express those of your animal guide. How do they move around the space? What are their gestures and expressions, how to they move their limbs, their spine, their head? Imagine they are moving with you and mimic their movements as you see them in your inner eye. Allow yourself to have fun and express yourself and your bodies' wisdom together with your familiar. Make a physical connection—let your muscles and very being explore that animal aspect within you.

After a few minutes—no more than ten the first few times you try it—thank your ally and ask them to return to the spirit realm. Stamp your feet on the ground. Without hyperventilating, breathe out great puffs of air to feel your connection is now gone. Clap your hands and feel your back, straight and tall. Feel that you once again fully inhabit yourself in your human form.

---

17. Robert Pitcairn, *Ancient Criminal Trials in Scotland, 3, part 2*, (Bannatyne Club: 1833), 607.

>) PRACTICAL (

WORKING WITH YOUR FAMILIAR

After you feel you have built up a good connection with your familiar or animal ally and can use this connection to sense it and move with it in the room, it is time to work with it in more practical ways. One of the best practices to develop relies on a certain amount of inner vision and seership in addition to a strong sense of presence in your day. This practice can be taken up by anyone willing to give it time and develop the sensitivity, as the familiar will do their best to communicate with you regardless of your psychic abilities or lack of them. When starting the day, call to your familiar to walk with you throughout the day and point things out to you when needed, such as warnings or suggestions on where to go or avoid. Ask your familiar for the same guidance with people and other decisions, such as which foods to buy in the market, which road to take home, and so on. That said, don't hand over all responsibility to your familiar—use your own common sense and make your own choices What you are doing here is developing an awareness of your familiar when it is out and about, and to heed warnings it gives you. Sometimes this will be the sight of the actual animal type during your day, behaving unusually, sometimes this will be a flash in your mind's eye, at other times it may be more subtle such as on product labels, street or shop signs, or represented in other ways. Equally you can develop the habit of calling them into your everyday life and increase your ability to heed their communications by carrying objects associated with your familiar, such as jewellery or a postcard image, or their likeness taped to your car dashboard.

Another way to work with your familiar in everyday life is to use its example when in need, such as embodying its behaviours and traditional associations as traits of your own behaviour. For example, a dog ally or familiar is a loyal friend and powerful guardian who fiercely protects whomever it cares about. Perhaps a dog coming to you is a suggestion to develop these qualities in yourself for a while. In addition, a dog ally can be called upon to guard the house at night and protect physical as well as spiritual and psychic boundaries. It can also be sent off to hunt down things you need such as information, objects, or even opportunities. Every animal familiar is different, but your work with them will always be dependent on your relationship, which should be one of mutual respect. Communicate with them in ritual as well as in your day-to-day life; interweave the communications of your mundane and magical sides, and always thank your familiar for its help. Make it regular offerings as well; ask it what it would like, or make offerings appropriate to its animal type.

Clan Animals

Many Scottish and Irish clans were represented by animals and used animals on their coats of arms, but it was also common for an animal to represent the clan's "soul," like an overarching spirit being or *riochd nan Daoine* (Scots Gaelic) which often appeared in dreams and visions to represent and embody the clan itself. At other times, the souls of dead clansmen were seen in animal form. It was quite common for ideas about spirits, ghosts, animal 'familiars' and even demons to overlap in Celtic cultures, the common experience of seeing spirits, with its roots in the pre-Christian cultures, survived and even thrived in various forms throughout the Christian era and beyond, continuing to this day.

> Those [ghosts] of persons about to die or newly dead, or of persons lying asleep, might appear as birds, moths, butterflies, bees, cattle, dogs, cats, mice, horses, frogs, pigs, deer, &c. In Arran to dream of certain dogs is to dream of MacGregors, MacAlisters or MacDonalds. Other clan soul-forms are bees (Mackenzies), plovers (Curries), doves (MacKelvies), cats (MacNicols and MacNeishes), pigs (Cooks and MacMasters), mice (Bannatynes), bulls (MacNeils), rabbits (Mackinnons), frogs (Sillars), sheep (Kerrs). The clan soul-animal or insect was called *riochd nan daoine* ("sign", "form" or "spirit" of the folk).[18]

---

18. Donald Mackenzie, *Scottish Folk-Lore and Folk Life: Studies in Race, Culture and Tradition,* (Read Books Ltd. 1933). Kindle edition, location 4202.

Animals in the Celtic tradition

Adder
Nathair (Irish, Scots Gaelic) Neidr (Welsh)

In cultures around the world, snakes have long been associated with transformation and earth energies. They are also often seen as representations of phallic power and fertility. Symbolising the soul's journey into the underworld and its return, they were closely connected to Druidry and featured on Pictish stones; they were also important to the Anglo-Saxons, for whom they represented the same things—transformation, sexuality, life force, and healing. St Patrick was said to have removed all the snakes from Ireland—a possible reference to the triumph of Christianity over the druids, as Ireland has no native snakes. The Welsh bards sometimes referred to the druids as *Naddred*—adders—presumably for their work with life force and magic. While snakes were often connected to ideas about male sexuality, they were also associated with goddesses as sacred guardians of wells and holy springs, especially Brigid, who later became Christianised as St. Brigit. Snakes were also closely associated with the horned god Cernunnos, who was often depicted wearing or holding snakes. Snakes were also depicted with eggs, and there is a close connection between these two forms of creative power—the Welsh druids were thought to have a precious stone known as the druid's egg, or the serpent's egg, which was their greatest treasure and most powerful magical tool. As an omen, familiar or ally, the snake teaches the importance of transformation, and of living close to the earth fully embodied, as a source of power and wisdom.

Bear
Béar (Irish) mathan (Scots Gaelic) arth (Welsh)

Bears are guardians of earth energy and deep primal, ancestral power. The Gaulish Celts worshipped a bear goddess, Artio, and a bear god, Artaois, most notably at the city of Berne, (Bear city) in Switzerland. An altar dedicated to the bear god has also been found in the town of Saint-Pé-d'Ardet in the *Vallée de l'Ourse* (*Valley of the Bear*), near Lourdes in France. Bears were always honoured as powerful animals since the earliest times, and possible signs of their veneration—especially that of the cave bear—have been found dating back as far as the middle Palaeolithic era, fifty thousand years ago.[19] The Celtic Caledonian bear was considered so ferocious it was greatly prized in Rome for fighting in the arena, and many chieftains and warriors wore bearskin as a sign of their ferocity and status. The legendary King Arthur, probably once a god, perhaps embodied by a pre-Roman British war leader, takes his name from the bear—*art*—as a fierce protector of the land who carries the power of the ancestors and the earth with him. Equally the Pole Star, part of the constellation the great bear, is seen as a guide and ally when traversing the underworld, when we find ourselves floundering in our lives, or through the dark northern winter months. For this reason, modern druids call the Winter Solstice *Alban Arthan*, the *light of Arthur*, to invoke his protective presence both in earthly and stellar form. The bear as an omen, familiar or animal ally calls you to remember your wild knowing, and to honour your ancestral roots. Protective and powerful the bear teaches about the balance between winter and summer as markers of our spiritual journey, and the balance between our instinctual knowing and our higher reasoning, indicating that both are needed to seek wisdom and self-knowledge.

Boar
Torc (Irish and Scots Gaelic) twrch, baedd (Welsh)

Boars were associated with warriorship and leadership across Iron Age Britain and Ireland, as well as northern Europe. They were deeply important to the Picts in what is now Scotland, and several famous carved Pictish stones have been found with beautifully designed boars upon them, bristles raised ready for battle. The Knocknagael Boar-Stone is a large slate slab with a beautifully designed carving of a boar. Above it is a disc and rectangle shape known as a "mirror case design" dating to the seventh century. The stone shows that the boar's cultural importance continued well into the Christian era. Elsewhere in Scotland, the famous boar stone at Dunadd stands near

---

19. Ina Wunn, "Beginning of Religion." *Numen* 47, no. 4 (2000): 435–436. http://www.jstor.org .ezproxy.uwtsd.ac.uk/stable/3270307.

where the kings of the Dál Riata were crowned. Boars were also popular symbols to decorate Celtic armour, and a helmet with a boar's crest was found in Wales. The boar symbolises fierceness and intimidating power; they can be very dangerous animals and to hunt the boar was a sign of great male prowess in former times. In the earliest Celtic period, the boar hunt may well have had ritual significance, and its mentions in the Celtic literature of Wales and Ireland give it mythic importance. Boar hunts in myth may have represented a journey into the otherworld, with the corresponding themes of life and death. Facing your fears and inner demons, represented by the fierce boar, may have been seen as yielding spiritual treasure upon the heroes return, transforming them upon return to the mortal world. The Irish Fionn cycle mentions *Formael*, a huge boar who kills fifty warriors and fifty hounds in one day. In the Welsh tale *Culhwch and Olwen*, two boars—*Ysgithyrwyn*, the king of boars, and *Twrch Trwyth*, the boar of Trwyth—must be killed for the hero Culhwch to be allowed to marry Olwen, the daughter of the giant *Yspadadden Penncawr*. Twrch Trwyth has a comb and scissors (perhaps symbols of an ancient goddess) tangled on his head that must be retrieved to groom the giant's hair. A boar as an omen, familiar, or animal ally teaches the qualities of bravery and leadership, as well as the benefit of confronting our own inner and underworld material to transform it and gain its power.

Fox

Sionnach (Irish and Scots Gaelic) llwynog (Welsh)

Foxes have long been considered creatures of wild intelligence and cunning. In the British Isles, these clever and elusive animals have often become the focus of rage by those who see nature as something to be controlled, tamed, feared, or even eradicated. And yet, as one of our last remaining predators, the harm they pose is almost non-existent, completely out of balance with the ferocity of opposition to them found in the countryside and the town. Despite this challenge, foxes have proven themselves to be highly adaptable animals who have found a way to survive even in the harshest of urban environments, where many wild animals could not. They bring with them the reminder that nature will always find a way. It was these qualities that made them so popular with the Celts, and they were taken up as tribal symbol animals with great enthusiasm. A Gaulish chieftain, Louernius, was known as son of the fox, and in Ireland the chieftains of the high status O'Catharniagh clan were known as Sinnachs, or the foxes. Lindow Man, an Iron Age body found in a peat bog at Lindow near Manchester wore a fox fur armlet among other details which suggested he was a high-status individual and possibly a ritual sacrifice. It may be that foxes themselves were once sacrificed by the Celts, as they have been found ritually buried in both France and England. A ritual pit in Hampshire contained one red deer and twelve foxes, suggesting a connection between the colour of their pelts and perhaps a magical significance to their red fur. As an omen, familiar, or animal ally, the fox teaches us about our relationship with wildness whether in the world around us or within. Cunning and adaptable, foxes carry an innate intelligence and can disappear into a landscape almost without trace but are also a depository for peoples fear and prejudices. If fox is your ally, walk softly and seek to be aware of what is around you.

Bull
Tarbh (Irish, Scots Gaelic) Tarw (Welsh)

Bulls symbolised great power and fertility in the Celtic traditions. The Irish once held the *Tarbh Feis*, the bull feast, as part of a ritual to determine who would be the next king, and they were closely associated with the thunder god Taranis, who was said to bring expansiveness and abundance, the great fertility of the sky down to the earth. Bulls represent potency and steadfast persistence in achieving goals over time. They are also territorial guardians of the earth. Symbols of wealth virility and power, bulls signify kingship in the sense that they encourage our inner sovereignty and the wise use of strength to overcome life challenges and achieve our aims, especially if they involve protecting or increasing the well-being of the family, tribe, or collective. If the bull or cow is an omen, familiar or animal ally, you will learn that strength is developed over time and should be used with honour and integrity as a source of power to support those around you as well as yourself. An animal of great nobility and abundance, the bull teaches the importance of generosity and endurance with regards to leadership and caregiving. We are reminded that those in power equally hold a moral responsibility to those around them.

Dog
Cù (Irish and Scots Gaelic) Ci (welsh)

The dog represents protection and loyalty, the companion. Dogs are always seen as guardians to the mysteries, capable of underworld travel. They are excellent allies to lead you through the otherworld and alerting you to danger and consuming negative energy. Dogs represent faithfulness and loyalty, fierceness and guidance. The Irish hero Cù Chulainn, the hound of Ulster, from the famous tale the Táin Bó Cúailnge (The Cattle Raid of Cooley) was named after a hound he killed, and a responsibility that he took on to be the faithful guard and protector of the people of Ulster against its enemies. There are several other famous hounds in the Celtic traditions such as King Arthur's hound Caball, and Dormach of the ruddy nose, the hound of the Welsh hunter god Gwyn ap Nudd. Gwyn and his hound lead the spectral wild hunt, the faery or otherworldly hounds the Cŵn Annwn, also known in some parts of the UK as the Wish or Wisked Hounds—a tradition Christianised into calling them Hell Hounds as the traditions of the faery hunt were subsumed into ideas of a demonic hunt that lead its prey to hell. If the dog or hound appears as an omen, familiar, or ally, you are called to learn the wisdom of loyalty and faithfulness in your relationships, as well as when to rescind that loyalty. Dogs are also powerful guides to assist in accessing the otherworld or underworld and protect you when traversing these realms in spirit.

Deer
Fia (Irish) Fiadh (Scots Gaelic) Carw (Welsh)

Deer and stags, closely associated with Cernunnos, are an archetypal symbol of the wild—graceful and powerful, they are utterly present to their surroundings and embody dignity and have a proud, regal quality. Seen as kings of the forest, stags are known for their beautiful antlers and their spectacular battles during the rutting season. Sexuality, power, independence, and integrity are all represented by the deer, who have been honoured in Ireland and the UK for millennia. Ritual deposits of antlers probably honouring the gods of the hunt have been found dating from the Neolithic era and even earlier. At Star Carr in Yorkshire, a great deal of archaeological finds dating to the Mesolithic era (the site was in use between approximately 9300 BCE and 8480 BCE) have been discovered, pointing to the ritual use of antlered headdresses, which have been fantastically preserved in the waterlogged peat. Elements of the veneration of deer and deer gods remain to this day. The famous Abbots Bromley horn dance, which takes place in September, ushers in the autumn with festivities and a ritual folk dance that uses antlers. The dance is a tradition dating to the eleventh century and illustrates the importance of the deer to British folk culture. In Ireland, the wife of the hero magician Fionn Mac Cumhail was a woman named Sadhbh, who had been turned into a deer by a jealous suitor. She was told she could be freed of her enchantment if she went to the Dun (castle) of Fionn, where she was magically turned back to her original human form. Fionn fell deeply in love with her, but she was tricked into her deer form once again. While Fionn searched for her endlessly he was only able to retrieve their son, Oisin, from the enchantment; Sadhbh was never seen again. If a deer comes to you as an omen, familiar, or animal ally, you are called to learn the wisdom of your heart as well as your sexual nature, and to learn how to carry the qualities of emotion and sexuality with grace and balance. Love and fertility are both in the realm of the deer, as is the quiet majesty of the wild. Learn to be still and silent, and feel your way forwards from your heart and central knowing core.

Wolf
Faolchú / Mactíre (Irish) Allaidh (Scots Gaelic) Blaidd (Welsh)

Wolves were always known to be teachers as well as guides in wild places. Often feared, wolves are actually shy, secretive animals who are fiercely loyal to their pack and their partners. They teach us about using our intuition and instincts. There were numerous Scottish clans that had the wolf as their totem, such as the MacLennans and the Macmillans. Wolves were favourite images for late Iron Age iconography, and they were often depicted with the horned god. The Gundestrup cauldron depicts wolves together with stags, a snake, and a boar. Wolves were once widespread in Britain and Ireland but were hunted to extinction perhaps in part due to the island nature of both areas. The last wolf was killed in Ireland in the late 1700s, some three hundred years after they were made extinct in England. However, wolves feature especially strongly in Irish mythology. The mythological High King of Ireland Cormac mac Airt was said to have been raised by wolves and know their speech, and he was said to have been accompanied by four wolves throughout his life. The war goddess the Mórríghan was said to turn into a red wolf, particularly in her battle against Cú Chulainn. And in the Fenian Cycle is a character named Airitech who has daughters who appear as werewolves. As an omen, familiar, or animal ally, wolves are steadfast friends who teach us to value experience and the learned wisdom of the body. We are called to trust our gut and animal senses, as well as our wild inner selves.

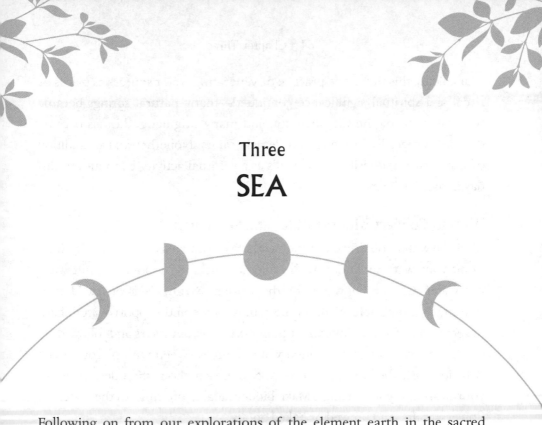

Three
SEA

Following on from our explorations of the element earth in the sacred Celtic triplicity of earth, sea, and sky, we now turn our attention to the element of water and sea that surrounds these lands, so often understood as a liminal access point to the Otherworlds and the spirits.

Water Magic

In the British Isles and Ireland, bodies of water, rivers and natural springs, wells and marshy liminal places on the landscape have been venerated since earliest times. Traces of ritual activity have been found to have occurred around bodies of water since the Neolithic era some six thousand years ago, dating to 4000 CE. One traditional practice was to make offerings to the spirit of the waters, such as stone axe heads and (later) bronze and iron swords, as well as other precious goods and items. Another common offering was items which took skill to prepare, such as large wooden containers of butter, known as bog butter. By the Iron Age, the spirits of the waters were considered to be female deities, with many rivers being called after their tutelary goddesses. It's likely this tradition was already thousands of years old by this time. The practice of venerating water sources as places of ritual and spiritual significance continued—many natural springs became the holy wells of the Christian era, and many original goddesses became demoted especially in Wales, into female saints. Nonetheless, the tradition of honouring and visiting holy wells as a spiritual activity continues to this day in various forms.

Ways to Connect with the Water and Sea Spirits

Bless the water you drink and cook with. Seek out wells and natural springs. Limit your water pollution with ecological cleaning products. Limit wasting water. Gather rainwater for the garden. Swim. Seek out wild river swimming where safe. Walk in the rain. Donate and support water charities, and campaign to limit water pollution. Seek out rivers and follow their courses. Dowse for underground water sources. Weep with sorrow. Weep with joy. Visit the sea. Sing to the waves. Learn about the tides. Listen to your heart and your feelings. Make biodegradable offerings to the water, of flowers, crafts, and brewed or baked goods.

Sacred Springs and Water Deities

Sacred springs and wells have long held a special magic, as entrances into the womb of the land, and the Otherworld in its various forms. Like ancient flint mines that have been found dating back to the Palaeolithic era, they were likely honoured as places of Chthonic or earth energy; home for spirits, ancestors, and gods; and were likely treated with some measure of fear and trepidation. By the Iron age Celts, they were places of ritual divination, and possibly sacrifice. The life of the tribe or community was dependent upon its water sources, which could bring healing or disease. As such, the spirits of the waters had the power of life and death over the people. Our dependence on water in the Western world may feel removed now from our immediate landscape with the invention of modern plumbing, but the water spirits have as much power over our lives as ever. As the world and our climate change, periods of drought or excessive rainfall can have devastating effects on our lives, and pollution of our water systems can cause terrible damage to wildlife, our health, as well as our connection and relationship to the water and other nature spirits that surround us. If we disrespect our environment, why should the spirits inherent in our environment respect us?

Our relationship with the water spirits can be mended and vastly improved if we give them our care, respect. and return to the ancient practices of making offerings and observing bodies of water as sacred, liminal places.

Gods and Goddesses of the Waters and Waves

To the Celts of the Iron age and Romano Britain, pools, lakes and rivers were all host to their own spirits and residing goddesses—archaeological evidence has given us some of the names of these deities and hints about their worship. Later medieval tales, especially in Ireland, are likely to have preserved some of this oral lore and tradition and have furnished us all with some vivid mythology, folk tales, and mystery teachings. Here is a list of some of the more notable water deities.

Lir/ Ler (Irish) Llŷr (Welsh)

Found in folklore and medieval tales most likely from earlier sources, Lir is most usually seen as an ancestral god of the sea, and is known best as the father of the sea god Manannán mac Lir who seems to have taken his place. Lir is also known in the tale "The Children of Lir," where his second wife, Aoife, jealous of his children turned them into swans for nine-hundred years. Symbols of poetry and the bardic arts, swans are sacred animals in Celtic myths; this tale may have teaching threads within it related to inspiration—known as *Imbas* in Irish—found through contact with the sea and otherworldly voyages, as the Celtic otherworld is often described as being found across the ocean. The Welsh Llŷr features in the collection of tales known as the Mabinogion, as the father of Bran and Branwen, and is probably the same being.

Manannán mac Lir (Irish) Manannan mac y
Leir (Manx) Manawydan fab Llŷr (Welsh)

Manannán mac Lir features widely in Irish mythology as one of the Irish gods in the Tuatha Dé Danann, like his father Lir. A guardian of the Otherworld, he is said to posess a sea-borne chariot drawn by the horse *Enbarr* ("water foam," lent to the god Lugh) and own a powerful sword named *Fragarach* ("the answerer"), and *féth fíada*, a cloak of invisibility. He is sometimes seen as a trickster and often leads characters through transformational experiences, especially in the tale of Cormac mac Airt. He is the king of the otherworldly "blessed isles" Mag Mell, and Emhain Abhlach, the Isle of Apple Trees, whose British equivalent is the isle of Avalon. On the Isle of Man, which is said to be named after him, he is seen as a god of the sea and as a trickster—a magician who was the first king of the island. He is also said on the Isle of Man to be the foster-father of the god Lugh.

Nechtan (Irish) Nuada (Irish) Nectan (British)
Nodens (Romano–British) Nudd (Welsh)

Nechtan features in Irish mythology as the god of the spring which is the source of the river Boyne, known as Nechtan's Well, also known as the *Tobar Segais,* or the Well of Wisdom, around which nine hazel trees grew, imbuing the water with their magical knowledge. He may be the same as the king Nuada of the Irish gods, the Tuatha Dé Danann, although in the collection of texts known as the *Dindsenchas,* (meaning "the lore of places," dating from at least the eleventh century) he is listed as the son of Nuada. Nuada is also known as Nuada Airgetlám (or Airgeadlámh, meaning "silver hand/arm") after losing an arm in battle, which was replaced with one of silver. Nechtan features in many folk tales relating to bodies of sacred water. In Cornwall, the famous St Nectan's glen, with its arch of stone and waterfall, was clearly a sacred place before the coming of Christianity, and St Nectan is most probably a version the same figure. In Wales, he is known as Nudd, and is the father of the god of Annwn, the underworld, Gwyn ap Nudd. He was worshipped as Nodens, the etymological source for Nechtan, Nuada, and Nudd, in Iron Age and Roman Britain, as a god of hunting, dreams and healing, and possibly fishing. A Romano Celtic temple to Nodens, at Lydney park, overlooking the Severn estuary between England and Wales, has been interpreted as a healing sanctuary, known as an *incubatio*—a place for pilgrims to dream of a healing remedy, or receive healing from the god via their dreams.

Boann

Boann is the goddess of the river Boyne in Ireland, and in Irish Mythology and the *Dindsenchas*, it relays that she was the wife of Nechtan, who forbade her to go to the waters of his well of wisdom. She broke his rule, walking around it counterclockwise, releasing the waters that became the river. Caught in the flood, she lost an arm, a leg, and an eye in the process—a particular disfigurement that is a recurring motif in Irish lore usually suggesting that the figure walks between the worlds and has otherworldly vision and ability, due to the other eye, arm, and leg being in the otherworld. In another version of the story, she drowns after washing herself in Nechtan's well to hide her infidelity after sleeping with the god the Dagda and giving birth to their son, Oengus. Boann means "white cow" (Irish: *bó fhionn*; Old Irish: *bó find*), and she is also seen as an earth and fertility goddess. As a goddess of wisdom, she is also associated with the hazelnuts which hang over Nechtan's well, imbuing it with wisdom. In the 2nd century CE, the Roman writer Ptolemy recorded that the river was called Bouvinda, which is derived from the Proto-Celtic *Bou vindā*, "white cow," illustrating the great antiquity of her reverence at the site.[20]

Sulis

Sulis is the local goddess at the thermal springs at the city of Bath in Somerset, south west England. Her name seems to relate to both the Old Irish and Proto Celtic words for sun, and eye, *súil*. She is associated with healing, but also with cursing, as archaeologists have found a great many lead curse tablets thrown into her waters, asking Sulis (and her Romano-Celtic

---

20. Thomas F. O'Rahilly, *Early Irish History and Mythology*, (Dublin, IE: Dublin Institute for Advanced Studies, 1946), 3.

name, Sulis Minerva) for assistance in avenging perceived injustices. Her temple, the roman baths, were called after her *Aquae Sulis,* "the waters of Sulis." Minerva, the Roman goddess with whom she was associated during the Roman occupation, was the goddess of wisdom and warfare, hinting perhaps at Sulis's associations also at the time. The thermal waters of Sulis are still flowing today, and are highly beneficial for easing things like rheumatism, as well as a host of more subtle malaises of the spirit and the heart. There is evidence that people came to Aquae Sulis for all sorts of complaints; women visited the springs to heal female illnesses and to help with childbirth, small model breasts have been discovered, which may be charms for breastfeeding, and the springs were also important for healing eyes—eye ointment was available, and there were doctors and eye specialists on site to help pilgrims. This powerful goddess was so popular, that she seemed to thrive under the Roman occupation, and is still revered to this day.

Coventina

Coventina may have been the most important water goddess in the north of England, during the Romano-Celtic period. Her cult was centred near Hadrian's Wall which separated what is now England from the kingdom of the Picts (now Scotland), at the northern limit of the Roman Empire. Her main site appears to be at Carrawburgh, where she was the personified spirit of a sacred spring and a pool fed by it. This was built up in 130 CE into a square walled enclosure that gradually gained more spiritual fame and significance over time, until the height of her cult in the third century. Her devotees tried to hide their worship of her, by placing flat stones over her shrine to hide and protect it in response to the Theodosian Edict of 391 CE, when Pagan rites were made illegal and temples were closed. Before this she was respected by the Roman empire and given the extra titles, *Sancta* and *Augusta,* Latin terms meaning *holy* and *revered.* Just as with the Cult of Sulis in Bath, Coventina received offerings of coins and also jewellery—rings, brooches, and interestingly, bronze face masks. There were also votive offerings of bone, glass, jet and shale. She is often depicted in stone reliefs as sitting with water nymphs or as a triple-aspected goddess.

It is thought she was once a beneficent "all-rounder" goddess who oversaw many areas of concern, not just healing, but was a caregiver and protectress to all people from the various trials of mankind.

☽ PRACTICAL ☾
OFFERINGS AND LIMINAL SPACES

Prepare an offering for the water spirits—something that took care and attention in its making, handmade and biodegradable, such as purpose made wicker sculpture, a bunch of flowers you have grown, or a wine or cordial you have made. Take your offering to a river, lake or the sea, whatever is nearest you, at dawn or dusk, liminal times of the day when the permeable boundary between the mortal and the spirit world is most accessible. Approach the shore and address the spirits—use your own words or try these to get you started. Something simple is fine.

"Spirits of the waters, please accept this offering, in friendship and respect."

Cast your offering into the waters with care and reverence. Bow your head and thank them for their many gifts to the human race.

☽ PRACTICAL ☾
MEETING THE SPIRITS OF WATER

This exercise can provide the first steps into connecting with the spirit of a water source near you. Treat it as a simple map for your connection and feel free to adapt it as you wish, although it is better after you have followed this exercise as written a few times. After a while, you will have begun to develop a connection with the water spirits attached to your chosen site, and can perhaps commune with them in a more spontaneous way, letting the spirit version of your locality and the spirits themselves guide and teach you as to how they like to be approached. But for now, use this as a simple template to get you started and initiate your connection.

Try this exercise at the water's edge, whether it be by a lake or spring or well, and sitting comfortably, close your eyes and take three deep breaths.

In your inner vision, or speaking aloud, call in your guides and allies to assist and accompany you, and announce your intention to meet the guardian water spirit of the place you are now sitting. Breathe deep and slow, feel your feet solidly upon the ground, and keep your back straight. Let your attention gently settle into your body, and then into the environment round you. What can you hear and feel where you are sitting? How does it feel physically, and more subtly, emotionally or energetically?

Now let your attention settle on the presence of the water around you in whatever form that is—river, spring, well, lake, sea, and so on. Can you hear the noises it makes, quiet or loud? Give it your full attention, just as if it were the voice of a loved one or a teacher. Trust that there is wisdom in its voice if you could but understand it. With your heart, in your inner vision, or (even better) out loud, call out to the spirit of the water and ask that you may meet the guardian spirit of the water. Say that you come in friendship and respect, stressing your good and respectful intentions and that you seek nothing but connection. Some bodies of water are places of resentment at least on the surface layers, so it is important to show your goodwill and respectful attitude. Slow down your breathing and wait.

After a while, you may sense a shift in your perceptions or get a physical sensation somewhere in your body. Look out for really subtle shifts, perhaps a whistling sound or a change of pressure in your ear … try your best not to get too stuck on how you imagine this connection to be, or how you think the water spirits should look—try to get out of your head and allow space for real connection to occur. This will take time and practice.

You may find images suddenly flash into your mind, or a feeling comes over you; equally, you may find your emotions shifting. If you are lucky you may get the clear sense of a presence, a being approaching you. Just as we can sometimes know when someone is standing behind us, if we are receptive enough, we may be able to sense their presence physically, don't worry if this doesn't happen to you quickly. Every person and every spirit is different, and it's a mistake to make too many presumptions on how your connection will form, as this can take us away from being truly present to the experience.

☽ PRACTICAL ☾
CLEANSING AND CURING

Holy wells and springs have long been used for blessings, curing, and cleansing. In Ireland and the British Isles these were places associated with specific goddesses, powers of place, and local gods called *genius loci* by the Romans who reported on them. Over time they became associated with Christian saints, many of the old traditions becoming transposed into the new religion. Getting to know the spirits of the water source you are working with and its history and traditions if possible, is always important.

One long lasting tradition is that of hanging clooties, a dialect word referring to strips of cloth upon hawthorn trees which often grow alongside wells and springs. These clooties were used for healing and removing ill wishes from a person by dipping them in the water and laving the sick person's body, after which they were draped upon the tree to take the illness or negative energies away. Hawthorn trees and holy wells often go together, and it is an interesting magical combination. Hawthorns are very good at working with the heart and our deeper feelings and their proximity to the energy of water as it comes out of the earth, literally emerging from the deep places, the liminal otherworldly places, into the light of day, means that they present a unique opportunity to seek deep healing and inner knowing. The hawthorn can help the healer, the person in need of healing, or any spiritual seeker to have greater knowledge of their own hearts, from which all transformation can begin.

Bathing regularly in fresh spring water, either at sacred wells and springs, or wild swimming where safe, are all excellent ways to draw the healing energies of the land and the waters into your body and soul, and to reconnect with your own sacred physicality. We are sensuous, vital beings, yet often the modern world locks us away from the intimate connection between ourselves and the land around us. Reengaging with water sources in a sacred way can return us to this blessed natural state.

If swimming in wild waters isn't an option, remember water even from the tap is part of the whole water system of the earth. All water is sacred; with the use of filters and a conscious attitude, we can improve the quality of our tap water immensely. We can also access spring water in bottles fairly easily, in which case it should be done as ethically and consciously as possible. Beware of spring water in plastic bottles, another pollution problem. Spring water is far better than treated water straight from the tap, but even tap water can be improved with filters, prayer, and blessing.

With that in mind try filling a bath at least partially with spring or filtered water and a handful of sea salt for an energetic cleanse. You can add to this by blessing the water yourself. Try this or use your own words:

"Blessed waters, you have travelled the earth and the sky, from the deep places to the most high … I ask that you bring to me the blessings of nature, of the earth, the rain, the rivers and seas … hold me as a baby in the womb of the land and grant me healing."

Gaze into the water; send it your love and care. In your inner vision, imagine its journey from rivers and seas and rainclouds till its time with you. See it as sacred. Scatter the sea salt and make another prayer, perhaps like this:

"May this be a bath of blessing and healing … thank you spirits of the waters!"

Well Dressings

Over time, the sacred wells of the Celtic pagan Iron-Age and Romano British period became Christian holy wells, usually associated with specific saints who may or may not have visited their associated sites. Many of these saints may have been adapted from the earlier gods and genius loci, the local gods associated with the area. Some wells or springs became associated with churches or monasteries, particularly in Wales where leaders of these religious organisations were often made saints after their death, but these places too usually had histories of sanctity long before the Christians came. The very fact that these sites have been in use for so long hint at their previous pre-Christian sanctity.

One traditional practice that probably pre-dates Christianity is well dressings—this is usually associated with Beltane or May day. A well or spring is decorated with flowers and other offerings, as well as candles, to honour the spirit of the well, which these days is usually a saint or the Virgin Mary. In the north of England, especially Lancashire, the practice of well dressing has become highly stylised with intricate designs worked out in flowers pressed into a large clay tablet. In this way the flowers stay fresh for several days, and they can be used to lay out a whole picture or symbol. The clay tablet in a wooden frame is then placed at the well as an offering. However, a more powerful practice is to build a relationship with the water sources in your own area over time and make smaller more personal offerings to its spirit—flowers are still good, but song and poetry as well as rubbish clearing are also poignant and something the spirits will recognise. In this way your connection can be simple, but heartfelt, and the act of pilgrimage to visit these water sources on significant times of the year, such as Beltane, continues this ancient practice without its modern Christian overtones.

Visits and pilgrimages at full moons or at times of personal crisis or crossroads are also important to build a close relationship between you and the spirits of such places. When we respect, remember, and reciprocate with the spirits of the sacred waters, we are not merely re-enacting an ancient practice—we are renewing it and continuing it with as much validity as at any point in the past.

Rainwater and Moon Water

In addition to spring water, we can also work with rainwater with a little care. Rainwater can be gathered in containers for use in gardens and a host of other things around the home. Often it is fine to drink, although this absolutely needs testing and checking first. Gather rainwater as well for use in blessings and magic, where it can be an alternative to fresh spring water, carrying the energies of the air and upper world rather than the earth. Rainwater is wild water—it has travelled far and brings messages from distant places, drawing from within us a reminder to be spontaneous, to surrender, and that nature will have its way and will always be stronger than us. Unlike river and spring water that we must travel to or seek out, rainwater comes to us, thrumming its insistent fingers on the window panes of our souls.

As well as its journey to us, where the water is gathered has great significance, and many Celtic and earlier sacred sites such as stone circles and high rocky outcrops in places like the Highlands of Scotland, and Dartmoor in England, have places where rainwater gathers and were probably used by those worshipping there from the earliest times. A common feature in British rock art is what are called cup and ring marks, small circular depressions cut into sacred stones, and it may be that these were sometimes places where water gathered and was used in a sacred manner, or the point of meeting where the water touched the stone made its own special magic. Not all of these type of rock carvings are positioned horizontally, but they often resemble the pattern of raindrops rippling upon the surface of water. At other places, depressions on the tops of standing stones and other features form natural bowls that gather water and charge it with their energy in a way that was surely intentional to those who constructed and originally used such sites.

Water is also charged and influenced by what is reflected in it. The light of the sun and stars, as well as the moon have a great part to play in water magic, and moon water especially is a powerful and useful wild potion.

) PRACTICAL (
PREPARING MOON WATER

The preparation of moon water is a traditional magical practice many paths have used since time immemorial. Moon water is used to bless and cleanse a person, space, or object; and it also serves as the basis for herbal potions and tisanes, vibrational essences, or any use that calls for water. It is also drunk to bestow or restore power, grant wisdom and psychic insight. Moon water is simply made but better when a strong spiritual connection to the moon has already been established.

Gather some fresh spring or rainwater and pour into a glass or pure silver bowl. Leave the water out where it will catch the light of the full moon overnight, with a prayer to the moon to charge and bless your work.

As with any magical working, your own spontaneity and relationship will serve you best should you include a prayer. What follows are my own words; you are welcome to use them in whatever manner you wish, until you discover your own.

"Lady of the moon, now your power is at its height, bless this water, pour your light upon it, lend your power to my magics ..."

If I had a specific need in mind for the water, I would mention this now; otherwise, I would thank the moon, and leave the water out to be gathered first thing in the morning, and bottled in a dark glass container.

Sometimes rather than using a silver container to make your moon water, a piece of silver- perhaps a piece of magical jewellery so long as it is pure silver- is placed in the water instead. The energetic compatibility between water, silver, and the moon are well established, and the silver will give the water added purity and cleansing.

If you intend to drink your moon water, make sure it is from a safe spring, or filter it appropriately first.

Water Scrying and Wisdom Seeking

Ancient druids sought wisdom and healing dreams by sleeping or meditating next to running water. Spending time just listening to the flow of a river, the roar or a waterfall, or the thrum of raindrops on the roof is an excellent way to tune out the conscious mind and access an altered state of consciousness in which deeper knowledge or spirit connection may be found. Time spent just listening to the roll of the waves by the seashore has the same effect and can almost hypnotise us or lull us to sleep in such a way that we are never fully aware of ourselves and can be struck by bright and powerful vision and insights. Running water can be described as having its own voice, sometimes a roar, and other times whispers, laughter, or singing. The sounds water makes vary infinitely and are never repeated. This is an excellent tool for divination, and it can help us to access the voice of the land and the gods themselves.

Try wild camping next to a river or waterfall or by the sea. Before you retire for the night, go up to the water's edge and make it an offering—a heartfelt gift perhaps of flowers, wine, or song. Call out specifically to the spirit of the waters present and ask it for its wisdom and connection. As you drift off to sleep, you may find you have sudden flashes of vision, or have significant dreams. Take care to write these down as soon as you wake and thank the waters for their gift.

Waterfall Initiation

Waterfalls especially have been used in the past as sites for initiation and rebirth- often the pools they create are called "cauldrons," suggesting a link to this purpose that has survived over the centuries. Bathing in such places can be dangerous for various reasons, but if sensible precautions are taken and you know the place well, it is possible to enact your own initiation and rebirth at these places at various times in your life—when you feel an ending and new beginning are upon you, or when you wish to dedicate yourself to your wild path.

By surrendering to the waters and allowing their power to wash us clean of our past and previous patterns and incarnations, we may emerge from the waters blessed and renewed, charged with their elemental power to set us in a new direction.

Water and Sea Spirits

Water and sea spirits in the Celtic traditions of Britain and Ireland come in a vast array of forms, and to cover each in any depth would be a book in itself. However, some stand out as more common types of faery and nature spirits or have especially famous tales and folklore attached to them. Many of these beings may well have been honoured as gods in times past, and some may have been known only since the Christian era or were always known more as spirits and faery beings.

Traditional Tales

The Blue Men of the Minch (Outer Hebrides)

Legends from the *Na h-Eileanan Siar*, (Scottish Gaelic: the Western Isles, also known as the outer Hebrides) say that there are three main groups of faerie spirits. Some say they fell from heaven, but earlier than that they were said to be the children of the ancient Celtic crone goddess *the Cailleach*. These were the Nimble Men and Merry Maidens (also known as the

Merry Dancers) who were giants who danced in the northern lights. The others were the fairies living beneath the earth in the faerie mounds, and the third, of the sea, known as the Blue Men. Sometimes also known as storm kelpies, the Blue Men of the Minch are traditionally mostly men, of human size with grey blue skin. The blue men favour the most dangerous waters, and delight in storms and wrecking ships. However, they were not always malicious; their leader, Shoney or Seonaidh, was given offerings of ale in return for the gift of seaweed to fertilize the fields. *Seonaidh* is Scots Gaelic for *Johnnie*, so what we have here is a generic or use name, as knowing his real name would have some measure of power against him, something the kelpies would never allow.

The Great Selkie o' Suleskerry (Orkney and Shetland)

"AN eartly nourris[21] sits and sing,
And aye she sings, Ba, lily wean![22]
Little ken I my bairnis father,[23]
Far less the land that he staps in.[24]
Then ane arose at her bed-fit,[25]
An a grumly[26] guest I'm sure was he:
'Here am I, thy bairnis father,[27]
Although that I be not comelie.
'I am a man, upon the lan,
An I am a silkie in the sea;
And when I'm far and far frae land,
My dwelling is in Sule Skerrie.'

---

21. Earthly breastfeeding woman, a nursemaid.

22. *Ba, lily wean*—howl, lovely child.

23. Little I know your father.

24. Staps—stays/ lives in.

25. Bed foot.

26. *Grumly*—troubled.

27. *Thy bairnis father*—your baby's father.

'It was na weel,' quo the maiden fair,[28]

'It was na weel, indeed,' quo she,

'That the Great Silkie of Sule Skerrie

Shuld hae come and aught a bairn to me.'

Now he has taen a purse of gould,

And he has pat it upon her knee,

Sayin, Gie to me my little young son,

An take thee up thy nourris-fee.[29]

An it shall come to pass on a summer's day,

When the sun shines hot on evera stane,[30]

That I will tak my little young son,

An teach him for to swim the faem.[31]

An thu shall marry a proud gunner,

An a proud gunner I'm sure he'll be,

An the very first shot that ere he shoots,

He'll shoot baith my young son and me."[32]

Selkies (Scottish)

Selkie is a dialect word for *seal* across Scotland and the Orkneys. It is also the name of the seal spirits, seal men and women who occasionally come to shore and shed their seal skins to dance upon the sand and sing beneath the full moon. In the old tales, Selkie men and women are always beautiful, and frequently fishermen fall in love with Selkie women and take them as wives. They hide their seal skins so they cannot transform again and return to the sea, but the selkie woman always finds her skin again in time, leaving her children and the forlorn fisherman longing for her return. Often the

---

28. "It was not well / good" said the woman.

29. Nursemaid's fee.

30. Every stone.

31. *Faem*—foam—sea.

32. The Great Selkie (or Silkie) of Sulle Skerry was first collected from a woman at Snarra Voe, Shetland, published by Capt. F. W. L. Thomas in the 1850s. It was later recorded in F. R. Childs anthology as "Child Ballad 113." (https://sacred-texts.com/neu/eng/child/ch113.htm.)

Selkie woman does return, but once a year, to see her children and teach them sea magic and healing potions.

Selkie men were said to be as handsome as the women and would entrance human women with their deep, dark eyes. Seal men would willingly leave their seal skins hidden and search for mortal women inland to seduce. At other times, women would seek out a Selkie lover by going to the shore at high tide and shedding seven tears upon the waves.

The Orkney antiquarian and folklorist, Walter Traill Dennison wrote a modern-day account of this practice in the *Scottish Antiquary* in 1893:

> She went at early morning and sat on a rock at high-tide mark, and when it was high tide, she shed seven tears in the sea. People said they were the only tears she ever shed. But you know this is what one must do if she wants speech with the selkie-folk. Well, as the first glimpse of dawn made the waters grey, she saw a big selkie swimming for the rock.
>
> He raised his head, and says he to her, "What's your will with me, fair lady?"
>
> She likely told him what was in her mind; and he told her he would visit her at the seventh stream [spring tide], for that was the time he could come in human form.
>
> So, when the time was come, he came; and they met over and over again. And, doubtless, it was not for good that they met so often. Anyway, when Ursilla's bairns were born every one of them had web hands and webbed feet, like the paws of a selkie.[33]

It was said that in Shetland, mothers would protect their daughters from the Selkies by painting a red cross upon their breast, and the selkies were feared, as were their almost identical cousins, the Finfolk.

---

33. *Scottish Antiquary* 1893, vol 7. JSTOR: https://www.jstor.org/stable/25516556?seq=1#page _scan_tab_contents.

The Finfolk

The Finfolk are another supernatural race living in the seas around Orkney and Shetland. They were said to be dark and terrible sea sorcerers who could come ashore and take human form at will. It was said they would steal away mortal young men and women to their homes at Finfolkaheem, their realm beneath the sea, or their magical vanishing island, Hildaland. The Finfolk had incredible seafaring skills and could control the weather to bring storms or calm upon the ocean with their magic. The traces of the Old Norse traditions may be seen in these tales, as the lands where the Saami folk lived in the far north used to be called the *emark*.

Sea Magic: The Tides and the Moon

Water and sea magic are closely connected to the cycles of the moon. This is due in part to an energetic resonance between the two. Water spirits have a great affinity to the moon and its shifting, subtle and mysterious energies, and they both have a strong effect on human emotions and psychic senses, the subconscious and our deeper intuitive awareness. Scientifically, we know that the movement of the tides, and by extension all bodies of water on the earth are affected gravitationally by the moon, and to a lesser extent by the sun. While scientifically the effects of the moon's proximity to the earth—which creates the tides- have a miniscule effect on lakes and smaller bodies of water, including the human body- it is still something that many people can feel. Meanwhile, the moon's effects upon the earth oceans is huge, causing energetic as well as physical tides that we can work with very effectively.

Loosely speaking, low tides can drain energy away from something—to banish, to cleanse, to lay to rest something which no longer serves us. We can also use high tides to bring in things- to bless, to make a project fertile, to draw in that which we wish to attract. It is useful to become aware of tide times in the seas nearest to our location (easily found online) as we needn't be physically present at the seashore to work with this, although it does help. Equally, it's worth noting that the period up to the seas highest and lowest points upon the shore will be the most effective time to perform magic—save the very highest and lowest turning points for things like spirit communion and divination or to overturn circumstances against you.

☽ PRACTICAL ☾
TIDAL MAGIC

When the tide turns and begins to go out and the moon is waning, take a seashell. Holding it to your ear, see if you can hear the sea within it. If you can, you may tell the shell all that you would be rid of and transformed in the coming month, be it problems, difficult relationships, ill health, difficult bills, or inner qualities that you need to surrender such as anger, sorrow, or grief. When you feel you have told the shell all that you need to let go of, thank it, hold it to your heart for a moment to honour it, and cast it into the sea.

The opposite magic can be performed when the high tide is coming and the moon is waxing to full. Stand upon the shore and call out to the moon and the waves, all that you would bring to you for the coming month. Cast your arms wide and breath in the power that is rising all around you. When ready, take a small bottle or glass phial and gather a little of the sea water. Bow your head in thanks to the mother of the ocean and the spirits of the sea and carry the water—the power of the rising tide—with you for a full month. After a month has passed, return the water from where it was gathered with gratitude.

The Spring Tide and the Tidal Race and Tidal Bores

The spring tide, also known as the king tide, is named not for the season but from the idea that it is "springing forth" during the new and full moons, which makes the waves and the tidal reach slightly higher. The neap tide occurs in between, at the quarter moons, around seven days later with the opposite effect. This means that the low tide is slightly higher and the high tide is slightly lower, owing to the sun and moon being at right angles from our perspective on Earth and cancelling out each other's gravitational pull. Needless to say, magic performed at the spring high or low tides will have added power than that performed during the neap tides, as we would be working with the natural rhythms. Therefore, the day or night before or (at latest) directly upon a new moon as the tide is going out or at latest near to reaching its lowest point is when to banish. The full moon high tide (or just before) is the ideal time to catch the rising energy or to attract. Meditating, journeying in your inner vision, or seeking spirit contact at these highest points at full moon and lowest at new moon is equally more powerful than during the neap tides in between.

A tidal race is when a high tide with a fast-moving current is forced through a constricted space and forms eddies, waves, and hazardous currents. A famous example is at the strait of Corryvreckan between Jura and Scarba off the west coast of Scotland. This tidal race flows over a series of underwater obstacles that combine to create the Corryvreckan whirlpool, the third largest whirlpool in the world. From the Gaelic *Coire Bhreacain*, corryvreckan means the *cauldron of the plaid*, said in folklore to be the cauldron of the Cailleach, the old woman of winter, who is said to wash her plaid within the cauldron before casting it over the land, creating a deep blanket of snow. The Corryvreckan is also said to be the home of the *na fir ghorma*, the blue men.

Working with tidal races and bores is highly powerful yet also quite chaotic—the forces of the sea are at their fiercest and have little interest in our concerns. Their reach is far and wide, however, so prayers and offerings for peace or healing for example cast (safely without risk of drowning!) into a tidal race may have a correspondingly far reach if the peace required is for a larger issue than an individual, such as the health of a community, or a prayer for the health of the sea itself. Casting magic intended for an individual's circumstances into a tidal race is not something I would recommend—the sea will have her own way, and an individual's needs may easily be lost in such power. The potential for a sympathetic magic kickback of a tidal race on one's life would most probably not be desired! As for a selfless prayer to the lady of the sea, that may go well, if she is willing.

A tidal bore is when the leading edge of a rising tide is forced up a river or narrow bay against the direction of the rivers current. This happens especially at spring high tides, most notably at the spring equinox (another powerful bore can occur at the autumn equinox as well). A famous example of a tidal bore is that of the Severn estuary between Wales and England. Working magically with a tidal bore runs along the same lines as with the tides generally—give away your cares or illness to the retreating tide. Even though it has reached far into your life, it may recede equally far. Similarly, a life in great drought may be refreshed and renewed with the blessings of a tidal bore bringing new life and opportunity.

Magical Tools from the Shore

The shoreline and seaside are great places to forage for natural magical objects and resources. These objects may grow or live in the area, or they could be washed up by the waves, originating across vast distances. Such objects often have magical attributes which connect them to land or animal/ plant and the sea itself, as the ocean marks them as its own. Sea-washed magical objects have their own unique qualities and power, and just as the motion of the waves and salt can affect their appearances, so the sea water and its lunar based movements will add their own energies to the mix. Equally, magical items may be washed in sea water for a strong cleansing and banishing of any negative energies, but care should be taken lest the sea water damage them while imbuing its own powerful magic. The following is a list of commonly found magical tools from sea and shore.

Mermaids Purses

Mermaids purses are small, hard, roughly rectangular objects that are often found along the tide line along the seashore. They are usually a dark brown in colour and are the now empty egg sacks of various kinds of shark. These strange and charming objects have a long tradition of use among sea witches for protection, wealth and fertility magic, and as powerful natural talismans. Associated with mermaids, those powerful, beautiful, and treacherous spirits of the sea, these are thought of as distinctly feminine magic, though they may be used by anyone. If you bring a mermaid's purse home with you, it's important to give the sea a gift in exchange such as a silver coin, a bunch of flowers, or a song. Always be environmentally conscious when making natural offerings; gifts of poetry and song are preferable to physical gifts. Although physical offerings were common in times past, leaving them requires careful planning if we choose them today.

One traditional use of a mermaid's purse was to bury it at the threshold of the home or bury one in each corner of one's property. Another was to gather the purses with other items into a charm bundle for fertility with herbs and other charms such as shells and seeds. Carrying or meditating with one may help you to access the realms of the water spirits, mermaids themselves, or the deep powers of the sea.

Seashells

Seashells are wonderful magical tools, a combination of earth and water magic, they are often thought to correspond to ideas around fertility and love magic, as well as beauty abundance and goddess work. Shells can be fantastic for holding water in ceremonies and rituals, and as special bowls for offerings. They can also be useful parts of wild divination kits.

Beautifully symmetrical scallop shells are sacred to the goddesses Venus and Aphrodite and are useful in love magic as part of a ritual or spell, to wear as a talisman or as part of a magical bundle. A spiral shaped nautilus shell reveals astonishing sacred geometry; the nautilus does not shed its shell but increases its size as it grows. Its shell is useful for magic related to growth expansion and renewal, as well as working with time and shamanic journeying as in the sacred triple spiral of the Celts relating to birth, death, and rebirth. The pointy spiral shell of the auger, which comes from a predatory sea snail, is considered both masculine and feminine, and its pointy horn shape suggests a correspondence with the planet Mars and male fertility. These wonderful shells are highly protective and are useful additions to wands and ritual garb. The vulvalike shape of the cowrie shell by contrast is highly feminine and useful for sex magic as well as fertility and calling in abundance. They are also popularly used in divination.

Starfish

Starfish are powerful magical creatures from the sea associated with good luck and protection, as well as connection to the stellar realms above—a beautiful example of "as above, so below." Starfish also serve as a sea witch's version of the pentagram. Pentagrams also symbolize the planet Venus and are thus useful in love magic. As these creatures are able to regrow their limbs, they are also useful talismans for healing and overcoming trauma.

Seashells and Starfish

Pebbles and Water-tumbled Stones

Water has a powerful effect upon stone, and tumbled rounded pebbles from the sea shore or river bed are useful allies that can be tools for divination when inscribed with words, runes, or ogham sigils.[34] They are just as powerful when felt and meditated upon as they have their own unique individual guidance. Tumbled pebbles can also be used to fill handmade rattles, and as decoration for your own sacred spaces and tools, carrying with them the energies of sea or river and earth.

---

34. For more information, see *Celtic Tree Magic: Ogham Lore and Druid Mysteries* by Danu Forest (Llewellyn, 2014).

One particularly useful stone found at the seashore is white quartz, which is often found amongst the other stones, and can be detected due to its glassier qualities than other white pebbles. This naturally smoothed crystal has often been found at Celtic and earlier Bronze Age archaeological sites, especially around graves or places associated with ceremony. Large versions of these were found liberally scattered around the Irish complex at Newgrange and have been used to restore its decorative entranceway. White naturally tumbled quartz has a very clear yet grounded energy that can be useful for scrying as well as healing; gathering a few stones when you come across them to give as offerings to sacred sites is a nice practice so long as it is done in moderation and with sensitivity.

❯ PRACTICAL ❮
SPELL FOR GOOD SEAS AND TIDES

Chant this traditional spell from the Western Isles to the new moon to ask for friendly seas and tides.

> Hail to thee, thou new lit moon
> I bend the knee, thou queen so fair;
> Through the dark clouds thine way be,
> Thine who leadest all the stars;
> Though thy light e'en find me joy-filled
> Put though flow-tide on the flood
> Send though flow tide on the flood.[35]

Banishing the Whale (Shetland)

An extraordinarily clever technique was used by Shetland fishermen to scare away whales, which were also known as *fjaedin* or *bregdie*. These huge beasts of the sea were something the fishermen feared almost above all else, as their sheer size had the ability to destroy their small wooden boats and drown them all. However, the main protection here was not through

---

35. Kenneth Macleod, *The Road to the Isles*, (Robert Grant & Sons, 1927), reproduced in Graham King, *The British Book of Spells & Charms* (Troy Books, 2015), 251.

magical means other than the good luck charm of a copper coin. Upon seeing a whale, the fisherman would hold the coin beneath the water, and scrape along its surface with the steel edge of his knife. It was believed that every boat so protected was safe from every whale, as they would waste no time in swimming as far away from them as possible as soon as this was done- due perhaps to the screeching sound of the metal upon metal having an unpleasant effect upon the whale's sensitive sonar hearing.[36]

---

bt36. John Spence Jr., *Shetland Folklore* (1899) reproduced by AlbaCraft Publishing, 2013. Kindle edition, location 802.

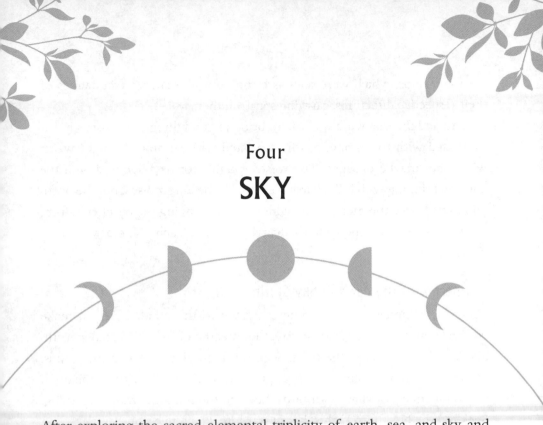

Four
SKY

After exploring the sacred elemental triplicity of earth, sea, and sky and examining the spirit presences and magic of earth and sea/water, we now turn our attention to the element and magic of air and the spiritual presences of the sky as understood in the Celtic cultures.

The Four Airts (Scottish)

In Scotland especially in the Highlands, there is the tradition of the *four airts* or directions, each direction being associated with a season, a wind, and a host of other lore. The east related to the spring, the south, summer, the west, autumn, and the north, winter. Much was made of moving in a sunwise, or *deisil* direction, to bless someone or an area, and processions were often held especially carrying fire, moving in a sunwise direction around the four directions to clear evil or bring in good health. Conversely, walking *tuaithiuil*, counterclockwise, or against the sun, also known as widdershins, was to bring in bad magic, or to banish something from an area, going against the turn of nature. The four airts were closely connected to the four winds, which were seen as bringing in the energy or qualities of their respective directions, carrying spirits in their wake.

East and the east wind was said to bring in good things, life, just as it was associated with the spring, south associated with summer brought warm winds, but maybe drought. The west brought storms associated with the autumn bringing with it the harsh weather of the autumn sea, but the north wind was feared the most, as the winter wind, bringing the bitter cold from the far northern ice, the wind that carried the Cailleach, the old woman of winter.

Connect with the Air and Sky Spirits

Hang windchimes. Get a barometer. Listen to the wind. Learn to make your own incenses. Sing. Chant. Breathe. Breathe deep. Collect fallen feathers. Watch the wind in the trees. Seek out high places. Watch the clouds. Minimize your air pollution, campaign for cleaner air. Fly a kite. Donate to a bird sanctuary or charity for birds. Look to the horizon. Watch lightning. Seek out the Northern Lights. Learn star lore. Get a telescope.

The Twelve Winds and Their Colours (Irish)

In the Irish tradition is the fascinating belief that the winds each have different qualities and even different colours. The direction of the wind that blew upon the day you were born is said to have particular significance, as it blows the air of your first breath into your lungs and carries with it wisdom and lessons; all the land it has travelled over thus gives you life in that moment and will carry you until the end of your days. The primary source for this belief comes from an amazing collection of poetry, the *Saltair na Rann* (Psalter of Quatrains) which are said to narrate the sacred history of the world. The *Saltair na Rann* is widely attributed to Saint Óengus mac Óengobann, of the late ninth century, but this authorship is disputed; much of the work may be far older.

Creation of the Winds with Their Colours from Saltair na Rann:

> King who ordained the eight winds
> advancing without uncertainty, full of beauty,

the four prime winds He holds back,
the four fierce under-winds.

There are four other under-winds,
as learned authors say,
this should be the number, without any error,
of the winds, twelve winds.

King who fashioned the colours of the winds,
who fixed them in safe courses,
after their manner, in well-ordered disposition,
with the varieties of each manifold hue.

The white, the clear purple,
the blue, the very strong green,
the yellow, the red, sure the knowledge,
in their gentle meetings wrath did not seize them.

The black, the grey, the speckled,
the dark and the deep brown,
the dun, darksome hues,
they are not light, easily controlled.

King who ordained them over every void,
the eight wild under-winds;
who laid down without defect
the bounds of the four prime winds.

From the East, the smiling purple,
from the South, the pure white, wondrous,
from the North, the black blustering moaning wind,
from the West, the babbling dun breeze.

The red, and the yellow along with it,
both white and purple;
the green, the blue, it is brave,
both dun and the pure white.

The grey, the dark brown, hateful their harshness,
both dun and deep black;
the dark, the speckled easterly wind
both black and purple.

Rightly ordered their form,
their disposition was ordained;
with wise adjustments, openly,
according to their position and their fixed places.[37]

    The twelve winds and their meanings may be unlocked by applying what we know about the Scots Gaelic four airts, and the seasons to which they are associated may have a similar origin that is now lost. While both of these traditions were recorded in the Christian era, they are likely to have pre-Christian roots and there were close ties culturally and linguistically between Scotland and Ireland. We may transpose the idea of the winds representing the seasons, into the metaphorical seasons of life from birth to death, placing the new life at the dawn, or northeast, and childhood or birth at the east, maturity in the south, age in the west, and death/rebirth in the north.

The Twelve Colours of the Wind

    East: purple, predawn light/birth
    Yellow, early sun/youth
    Red, stronger sun/adolescence
    South: white, mid-day light/maturity
    Green, growth/fertility

---

37. *The Saltair Na Rann* attributed to Oenghus the Culdee, ninth and tenth century. Eleanor Hull, ed. *Poem book of the Gael,* Chicago: Chatto and Windus, 1913, 5–7. https://archive.org/details/poembookofgael00hulliala/page/4.

Deep green, mature growth
West: dun, sunset/first touches of autumn
Grey, bones/autumn skies
Brown, tilled earth/roots
North: black, death/the void
Deep blue, first stirring
Speckled/light blue, the first coming of the light

Calling In the Winds

There are many ways to work with the many coloured winds; by their nature they invoke our creativity and inspiration, so they are limited only by our vision. Here is one way to work with them to seek balance and an interweaving of their blessings with you, and another to work with them individually.

❭ PRACTICAL ❲
WEAVING THE WINDS

If you can, seek a high place under a wide-open sky. Call in your guardian spirits, familiars, and spirit allies. Stand tall and take some deep breaths to calm and centre yourself. Turning to the east, use your voice to call the purple east wind to you. Don't worry if you aren't a singer, or are unsure of what to say—just use your breath, to sigh, whistle, intone, or make any noise as loud as you can. Call out to the west wind with your heart and intention. You might like to try the first syllable of one of the words for inspiration, *Imbas* in Irish, so the sound *eeee*. The point isn't to worry about how you sound but instead to open up your airways and vocal cords and make a tangible, physical call out to the fresh wind. Feel free to take a breath and make your noise again or to hold your note, just as you feel.

As you make your call to the wind, visualise it coming to you through the air, and across the land as an enlivening, ever new current of purple wind with a thread of blue upon one side of it and a thread of yellow gold upon the other side, the three together carrying with them all the energy of the east wind and its quick and bright intelligence. Breathe this light into your lungs and your whole being. See it blowing within and through you.

After a while when you feel ready, turn to the south and repeat your call. If you are using *Imbas,* use the next syllable, *emmm.* Visualise the warm south wind coming to you, carrying with it the steady heat of summer and the surety of adulthood, of finding things established and growing. See the south wind coming as a current of white-hot air with a thread of red upon one side and a thread of fresh green upon the other. Breathe the south wind into your whole being, and see it weaving and turning about you, blending and circling, together with the wind from the east.

When you are ready turn now to the west, and call to the west wind, as before using any sound which comes to you, or *baaa* for the next sylla-ble of *Imbas.* See the dun-coloured west wind of autumn and fields ripe for harvest coming to you, with threads of deep green and grey on either side, carrying with them the wisdom of fruition and experience and the deep knowing of the heart. See this west wind weaving in with the winds from the east and the south, all swirling within you.

Now turn to the north and the black wind of winter. Feel the chill of the endings and the silence of death, as well as the shimmering of the stars in a velvet night sky. Breathe in this wind of infinity, with the brown threads of the rich earth and the deep blue of space, carrying with it the wisdom of the ancestors and the spirit world. Call in the north wind, as you feel, or with the final syllables of *Imbas, sssss.* Bow to the north wind, acknowledging that we all must go with the north wind when our time has come. See it blow-ing through you, and weaving with the other three, till they swirl and bloom within you.

After a time, give your thanks to the north wind, and turn to the east once more. Take a step backwards, to a central spot and verbally give thanks to each of the winds and see the colours settle within you to still-ness within your heart. Take three deep breaths, and bend for a moment to place your hands on the earth, to signal the completion of the ceremony, and bring you back into being fully present in the world.

You may like to record your experiences in a journal.

The Coloured Winds for Magic

When you seek to do some magic or make a prayer, consider for a moment which wind would carry your wishes out into the world- purple perhaps for a fresh start or seeking a new way of looking at a problem. Call in the south wind perhaps for love or to find the strength to achieve your aims; call on the dun wind of the west to bring you healing and harvest. Call in the north wind to guide lost souls or carry prayers to those who have passed over.

When you have chosen the wind you want to call, repeat how you called to that particular current in the wind weaving exercise. Having created a sacred space first and calling in your allies, especially an ally from the air spirits, call out to the appropriate wind and visualise it coming to you, as a powerful and sentient being, and ask it for its assistance. Such magic is not suited to harmful or negative magic or for seeking vengeance or acting on jealousy or control over others. To ask the winds when your intentions are unkind would not go well and should be avoided at all costs. However, if your request is just, even if it is just for yourself, they may agree to assist you. Give them your thanks and make them an offering of incense or song in friendship for their help.

Wind Divination

It was a practice in the Scottish Highlands and Western Islands to divine the coming year by the direction of the wind at *Hogmanay* or New Year's Eve. This particular wind was known as *the old wind*, (ghaoth dhfhàgas à Choluinn) and it would thus be the prevailing wind as the new year began. There was a saying that accompanied the prophecy:

> South wind—heat and produce,
> North wind—cold and tempest,
> West wind—fish and milk,
> East wind—fruit on trees.[38]

---

38. Campbell, *Witchcraft and Second Sight in the Highlands and Islands of Scotland* orignally published 1902. AlbaCraft Publishing, 2012. Kindle Edition, location 2651.

☽ PRACTICAL ☾
SEEKING AN AIR SPIRIT

Try this exercise to make connection with the spirits of the air and wind, and to gather back to you the first breaths you ever took to reinvigorate your spirit. This practice is best performed on a breezy day.

First if you can seek out a high place, a hilltop is ideal, somewhere you can see for a large distance to the horizon is perfect. Otherwise, if you must work indoors, open all the windows and let the air in as much as you are able.

Stand tall, and feel your feet on the ground beneath you. Stretch your spine gently by raising and opening your arms as if to embrace the sky. Take three deep breaths. Turn to face the east and take a really large deep breath of its air. In your inner vision, see all the air ahead of you to the east. Now turn to the south and do the same, breath in deeply the air of the south. Now turn to the west, and do the same, before repeating in the north. Feel yourself to be a central point in the middle of the four airts around you.

Close your eyes and feel the wind. Where is it blowing from, which direction? Ask yourself: is it cold, warm, wet, dry? Where do you feel it has come from? Call out to the spirits in the wind, thank them for their presence, for all they bring. Feel the wind against your body, against your face as a living presence or presences.

Call out and ask that a guide and ally of the wind come to you now, a friendly spirit to advise you. In your inner vision, feel one come to you. They may be calm and clear in your mind's eye, or they may be curious and mutable. They may take any form. How do they seem to you? How do they feel?

Ask the wind spirit what it is like to be one with the air. Become aware of it as an endless ever moving presence touching all things.

Ask the wind spirit to gather to you the first wind that ever came to you when you were born. You may see yourself take flight with the spirit at this point, soaring over the land to the place and time when you came into this world. See the wind as it moves across the land there. What was its direction? What was its nature?

Ask that this wind return to you to breathe new life into you at this time. See yourself surrounded by and breathing in its fresh invigorating presence. What are the gifts this wind brings to you? Thank the wind and take joy in your connection.

After a while return upon the wind back to your body, and take some slow breaths, feeling the air in your lungs return you to your physical form, making you aware of your chest and your belly, of the heart pumping within you.

Take heed when the wind blows from the direction you have discovered was your origin, for it will bring you gifts and align you to your purpose here.

An Gaoithe Sidhe: The Fairy Wind (Irish)

Sudden localised whirlwinds and singular gusts of wind were often called *An Gaoithe Sidhe* and were believed to be caused by the faeries, especially those which occurred in a small corner of a field that picked up tufts of grass or hay, or where the other end remained still and calm. Sometimes they were seen as blessings, and as the faeries helping the farmers with their labour, and at other times they were treated with fear and thought to bring illness and bad luck. The fairy wind was said to be especially powerful, capable of ripping the roof off a house if those within it had angered the *sidhe*, or if they were defending their treasure or lands. The faeries are well known to consider any patch of land with a rath upon it to be their own and while they were thought to bless the people who owned such lands and left them alone, they were also thought to take their own portion of the crops that grew near them.

If it was a faery whirlwind, weather lore could be divined by its direction, and it was said that a clockwise wind foretold of rain, while a whirlwind that gathered up small knots of grass or crop would foretell a harsh winter ahead, as it was a sign the faeries were gathering in extra harvest to see them through.

Children were taught to fear the faerie winds, that they would no longer grow if they stood within them. However, it was also common practice for those afraid of whirlwinds or wishing to prevent the faeries carrying something away with it to throw an iron horseshow or knife within it to neutralise the magic.

If you see *An Gaoth Sidhe,* seek the advice of your familiars and your inner vision as to what it is the faeries are doing—are they friendly, or have they been angered at all? Greet the whirlwind with all due respect and bless its passing.

Faery Whirlwind

The Language of Birds

While birdsong is beautiful from a human perspective, it represents a whole world of communication beyond our awareness—sometimes territorial, to intimidate other birds off their patch, or to attract a mate. However, their language can be used to help us identify different types of birds in our area, as well as what other animals may be nearby. This natural awareness and experience can only help your work with the bird spirits and heed their communications all the clearer.

Ancient druids, Romans, and numerous other spiritual and magical paths over the years have used the flight of birds as a means to divine wisdom from nature and even make prophecies or augury from their movements. There are numerous ways this divination may be done, but central to all is the ability to be connected and at peace in a natural environment. To become successful, some prior work should be done to become a still observer in nature. Knowledge of the birds in your area and any folklore attached to them is also useful, but not as important as the ability to become fully present in nature.

) PRACTICAL (
BIRD DIVINATION

Find a place in nature to sit quietly in complete silence, remaining as still as is comfortably possible for at least half an hour (longer if you are able). Choose somewhere with good visibility around you, ideally in the woods or park where many birds are likely to be present. Before you sit, decide upon your question, then sit down and wait until you hear birdsong before speaking your question aloud, to the air, and all things present. Slow your breathing and feel the earth below you and the skies above, and just wait and watch.

What you are looking for is an answer which will come to you, not using verbal language, but by natures gesture. The flight of birds, their song, their movements towards and away from you and how they interact with each other will be your response. Interpreting this takes some sensitivity and intuition sometimes, rather like reading someone's body language. Here you are reading the body language of nature to guide you. You may see the progress of the situation you are asking about played out symbolically before you during the time you sit, you may equally find something occurs which gives a more dramatic individual statement, it will all depend on your question, and the answer nature offers you. Give it time, practice it regularly, and gradually you will be able to perceive clearer and clearer signs to guide you.

Another way to divine using birds is to begin your day by asking the spirits for a sign, perhaps in a short simple ceremony, or just while standing at your threshold before stepping out into the world for the day. Ask aloud and be as specific as possible. Look out for any birds that cross your path during the day, and interpret your answer in relation to the lore of the different birds. This is easier if you see one of the more well-known birds with more folklore attached, but let your intuition be your primary guide; interpret the bird's movements and the context in which it appears. What body language is nature expressing in the moment the bird appears?

Birds in the Celtic and British traditions
Owl
Cailleach Oiche (Irish, Scots Gaelic) Ulchabhán (Irish)
Comhachag (Scots Gaelic) _Tylluan (Welsh).

The owl's name in Gaelic, *Cailleach Oíche*, or the crone of the night, tells you a lot about its nature and reputation. Able to see into the dark the owl is associated with psychic senses and seeing spirits, as well as wisdom and knowledge. The owl shows you the hidden side of nature, and helps to build an awareness of the otherworld. Frequently seen at twilight, the in-between time, when the faeries and other spirits of the land are also most often seen, she teaches about walking in balance between this world and the other, and carrying what she has learned by travelling to-and-fro. The owl is an excellent ally or familiar for all sorts of magical and occult training, and for seeking initiation from one state to another, and is a powerful omen bird. The owl may warn of death, or the ending on one way of being, but she is also a powerful guide in the underworld, showing lost spirits the way, or showing the living how to navigate deep earth energies and the deep subconscious aspects of our inner selves. The night huntress is closely associated with the Welsh goddess Blodeuwedd (*Flower Face*) who is turned into an owl, which may be the other side of her nature as a goddess of the wild bounty of the land.

Raven

Fiach dubh (Irish Gaelic) fitheach (Scots Gaelic) Cigfran / Brân (Welsh)

The raven is a bird of fate and prophecy. She offers protection through troubled times but is also an omen associated with troubles and difficult points in our lives, reminding us that these are part of the normal weather in any lifetime. Ravens urge the use of truth and honourable conduct, being aligned to the currents of sovereignty within ourselves that demand a high standard of behaviour for the gifts of prophecy and wisdom to be opened up within us. Closely associated with the Irish war and sovereignty goddess the Mórríghan, she is also associated with the Welsh god Bran and his sister Branwen, the white raven. When he was killed, Bran ordered that his head be sent to White Mount in London, where it would guard the realm and warn of danger. As long as it remained it would keep all of Britain safe. In time, the Tower of London was built there, and the famous ravens of the tower (remaining to this day) were installed to honour this in the Christian era. It was said that after his death, King Arthur was turned into a raven, and in Somerset it was custom to doff or tip your hat to ravens as a sign of respect for the king. The god Lugh or Lud was also associated with ravens, who warned him of the approach of his enemies the Fomorians before the second battle of Magh Tuireadh. The association of ravens with war is also seen in their uses as totems for Celtic warriors who decorated their armour with raven imagery. Raven as an ally or familiar calls you to seek deeper wisdom, and marks times of especial significance, justice and fate.

Eagle

Iolar (Irish) Iolair (Scots Gaelic) Eryr (Welsh)

Eagles are closely associated with the upper world and the sacred high places of the Celtic tradition where mystics would seek vision and enlightenment from the gods. Scottish clan chieftains and the old kings of Ireland used to wear eagle feathers in their hats as signs of their status. Another Gaelic name for the eagle is *Suil-na-Greine*, which means *eye of the sun*, and it has long held solar associations of power, vitality, and wisdom. From a heightened perspective, the world can look very different, so the eagle also represents both the intellect and gaining an overview of life. The eagle is one of the four most important and frequently mentioned birds in the Irish and British traditions—the others being swan, crane, and raven. In the Welsh tale Culhwch and Olwen, the eagle of Gwernabwy is named one of the oldest animals, younger only than the great salmon, who knows the secret place where the Mabon (the divine youth symbolising hope and renewal) is imprisoned. In the Irish Voyage of Maelduin, it is recounted how Maelduin and his men watch an eagle dive into a secret lake and be renewed. These tales offer insight into how the upper world and the realm of the mind need to access the depths and the emotional qualities of water and the lake, to seek balance and to have their wisdom refreshed. The eagle is also mentioned in the Mabinogion, in the tale of Math ap Mathonwy where Lleu Llaw Gyffes, the husband of Blodeuwedd, is turned into an eagle upon his murder. Lleu is a Welsh version of the Irish god Lugh, and is turned back to his human form by the wizard Gwydion. The eagle as a familiar or spirit ally encourages you to rise above and seek inner sovereignty, courage, nobility of spirit, and emotional renewal.

Crane
Corr (Irish and Scots Gaelic) Crëyr (Welsh)
The crane is a deeply sacred bird in the Celtic tradition; to hunt or eat its flesh was taboo. Said to be able to predict the weather and able to sit still for hours, it teaches mindfulness and being fully present in the world yet separate from it in a deeply meditative space. An Irish tale tells of how a lonely crane lives on the island of Inishkea near county Mayo, where it has lived since the beginning of the world and will stay until the world ends. Cranes are associated with the ancient crone goddess the Cailleach, who's tradition of veneration may be the oldest in the whole of Ireland and the British Isles. She teaches patience and longevity and is credited with the creation of many ancient megalithic sites across Ireland and the UK. She is also said to become an old woman in winter and be renewed with the spring. The crane and its associated bird, the heron, are both associated with ancestral knowledge and spirit contact, able to fly to the underworld and return,

repeating the cycle of life, death, and rebirth. The sea god Manannan had a crane skin bag, the *Corr-bolg*, in which he carried deeply sacred magical tools and the crane bag in the modern period has become a bag kept by druids in which they kept their ogham sticks for divination and magic. The crane or heron as an omen bird of familiar spirit shows you secret knowledge and is a messenger from the spirits, asking you to listen to your finer hidden senses.

Swan
Eala (Irish and Scots Gaelic) Alarch (Welsh)

Swan is the bird of the bards and poets, bringing the qualities of love and soulfulness to all they touch. Swans represent the soul's journey to the otherworld in search of inspiration or true love. Creativity is seen as stemming from the otherworld, or faery in the Celtic traditions, and the swan is the bird of inspiration, drawing this creativity up into the mortal world. The swan features in many tales in the Irish tradition especially; it was once traditional in Ireland to say, upon spotting a swan, "My blessing with you, white swan, for the sake of Lir's children!" Lir was the god of the sea, and a king of the Irish gods, the Tuatha De Danann, who had four beautiful children, three sons and a daughter. They had a stepmother, Aoife, who was jealous of them, and she turned them into four white swans, for four hundred years. When the spell was finally broken, the children returned to human form only to die instantly of old age. While the crane is associated with carrying souls the swan is often associated with the soul itself, and the tender heart which can see the truth of things. It is this deep soulful and heart wisdom which opens the way to inspiration, and swan's skin and feathers were used to make the bards cloak, the *tugen*, for this purpose. A swan as an omen or familiar spirit will be a message to your heart, a call to take heed of your deeper feelings and your inner purpose.

Hawk
Seabhac (Irish Gaelic) Seabhag (Scots Gaelic) Hebog (Welsh)

Hawks and falcons, like eagles, are considered to be solar birds, concerned with the upper world and nobility. However, while the eagle, as perhaps the greatest of the birds is associated with kingship, hawks and falcons in Celtic tales often have ancestral connections, or are associated instead with knights and heroes. The nephew of king Arthur, Gawain, who challenges the Green Knight is also known as *Gwalchmai*, the hawk of the May, and Galahad, the son of Lancelot, was called *Gwalch-y-had*, the hawk of summer, embodying the highest heroic and chivalric standards, in search of the grail. Hawks are also closely connected to ideas about far seeing, and attention to detail—to have *eyes like a hawk* is to notice everything around you and all the implications of a situation as if viewing something from above. In medieval times, falconry was a popular sport and hunting technique, and there was a strict hierarchy for birds—falcons were used by kings and dukes, the merlin hawk was for ladies, the sparrowhawk for priests, while the goshawk was the only bird yeomen were allowed to use. Therefore, when the falcon is mentioned in the ancient tales, we know that its associations are with the highest nobility, the worthiest characters, and the highest principles. In the Irish tale the Hawk of Achill, the hawk is the oldest of birds, who has seen the world from its earliest times. And in the great Irish mythological text *The Book of Invasions (Lebor Gabála Érenn)*, Fintan the great shamanic ancestor, becomes a hawk, as well as a salmon and an eagle in his long life, carrying the ancestral knowledge of his people into the future. But while these are birds of nobility and pride especially in our heritage, it must be remembered that the hawk is also a dangerous bird, able to hunt other birds and mammals easily. It is clear in its purpose, not swayed by feelings. As such, it may be associated with the mind and the spirit more than being incarnated in this world. Its lessons are more about the importance of rising above and the wisdom a greater overview grants the seeker. However, the hawk is also aggressive—it can be a ruthless predator at will and is a formidable foe. A hawk or falcon as an omen bird or familiar spirit urges you to keep your wits about you and be clear in your purpose, while holding pride in your power and accomplishments, and knowing your worth.

Néladóracht: Cloud Divination (Irish)

It's said that the ancient druids had a whole host of star lore, and weather lore, connected to their long-standing meditations upon the skies, but now most of this knowledge is lost, or only fragmentary. One such fragment, is the practice of Néladóracht, or cloud divination. Its hard to know how old this practice is as most of the written evidence for it comes from Irish texts of the eleventh century, but we know that all that has survived is but a tiny fragment of what was once known about druidic practices, and the remaining fragments are beautifully tantalising.

The main sources for our knowledge of Néladóracht come from three places; the Middle Irish life of Saint Columba/ Colum Cille of Iona, produced around 1150, the collection of secular tales of Fionn mac Cumhail, known as *Acallam na Senórach, Tales of the Elders of Ireland*, and in the Stowe version of the *Táin Bó Cúailnge*—a late medieval redaction of the famous raid. The source which gives us the most information on Néladóracht is found in *Acallam na Senórach*, where Fionn consults his druid Cainnelsciath on what some ominous clouds portend and is answered:

I see a cloud clear as crystal,
Hang above a wide doored *bruiden* (hostel),
There will the chief of a band one day shall be,
When the chalk flies from shields as they are riven.
A cloud of grey, foreboding grief,
I see in the midst between the other two.
That for which the ravens lust
Shall come of the event
When there is glint of weapons in their play.
A crimson cloud than which blood unmixed
Is not more red,
I see there poised above the two.
If battle there be, and so there will,
The hue of ruby gore
Will prove to have portended wrathfulness.

That bodies must be tortured,
And great hosts perish in the early day:
O King of Cliu that knowest every day;
the three clouds which I see foretell.[39]

In this work we see an occurrence of the powerful three-fold symbol that appears so often in the Celtic tradition, together here with an example of the magical motif of the combination of red white and black/ grey, as a foreteller of prophecy.

The colour red tends to signify blood and battle, as well as the earth's vivid life force, the feminine principle (remember that the goddess Mórrighan oversaw the battlefield), and the realms of faery. White is a colour associated with the spirit realm and upper world, as well as the male principle: note how the druid Cainnelsciath associated this with the fate of the lord or king. The colours red and white are often combined or opposed in Celtic tradition, more so than black and white. Black/ grey here is *"the colour of crows and trickeries"*—crows are birds associated with death, fate or destiny, and the underworld.

This example of the uses of cloud divination is of course highly dramatic, being part of a hero tale. However, it serves as an example of how we may approach the practice today. It's possible to perceive signs and omens in all sorts of things when in a purely meditative state, and cloud gazing is a perfect opportunity to let consciousness expand and float free for a while.

The trick is to keep your mind as receptive as possible whilst having a store of symbolism (traditional or your own), to help you interpret what you see and make the practice useful. For this I advise letting your imagination expand and make free associations between things intuitively. Let your own stream of consciousness lead you to the information you seek, and take heed of wider, time-honoured signs and portents that may point to meanings concerning the larger aspects of society around you. Balance

---

39. *Agallamh na Senórach* translated by Standish Hayes O'Grady, in *Silva Gadelica, a collection of Tales in Irish*, (London: Williams and Norgate, 1892), 261.

in all things! The sky may help your inner senses tune into wisdom, allowing you to feel the threads of the great web that connect you to all creation. You may learn how to discern the pattern and vibration of these threads—the key to all divination on one level—but the sky is a vast body in its own right. It equally may show you things relating to the wider world when it chooses…it's a two-way relationship after all.

❯ PRACTICAL ❰
CLOUD SCRYING

First decide on your question. It needs to be clear and succinct, something easy to hold in your mind with enough detail to be clear on its implications, but not so complicated that it is a distraction to tuning in.

To perform the scrying, go somewhere with a clear and wide view of the sky; a high place like a hilltop is best, but any place with a good view of the sky is fine.

Settle yourself comfortably, lying on your back or sitting, and take some deep breaths. Call in your allies and guides to assist you, especially air and sky allies you may have called already.

Now rest your eyes on a patch of sky—it needn't be a wide panorama unless you are lucky enough to work where you have a wide dramatic view, but it is important your head remain still and take in only that which crosses your vision. Sometimes a small patch of sky works best, but it all depends on where you are.

Now breathe with that patch of sky—imagine your breath as a cycle of energy between you two as you breathe into it, and breath it in by turns. When you feel ready, ask your question to the sky out loud.

Gazing at your chosen patch of sky, let your eyes rest and settle with the mood of the sky. Give yourself plenty of time—at least half an hour—and see what shapes and movements you can detect. Sometimes you will see animals, beings, or symbols; at other times, the movement of the clouds and their relationship with each other and the world about them will be your answer. Discerning the messages of the clouds is more of a felt and intuitive art rather than anything logical or rational. Ask yourself: how do you feel? What do you feel they are saying?

When you feel you have received your message or it's time to end the exercise, take a moment to deeply thank the sky and the clouds for their help as well as your guides for their assistance. Take a moment to wiggle or tap your feet upon the ground to really bring your attention back to the ground and your body. Consider also eating something small to really feel earthed. You might also like to record your experiences in a journal.

Weather Magic

> On leaving the land the boat was always turned with the sun —from east to west—never in the opposite direction, which was termed widdershins. The movements of witches were always made against the sun, and by whirling a wooden cap in water or a hand-mill on a bare looder (wooden bench on which the mill rested), they were supposed to be able to raise the wind like Furies, and toss the sea in wild commotion capable of destroying anything afloat, from a cock boat to an armada.
>
> JOHN SPENCE, *SHETLAND FOLK-LORE*.[40]

Celtic myth, folklore, and magical history are full of stories and accounts of witches being accused of bringing storms, winds, and rain. Our traditional witchcraft, based upon a close relationship with the faeries, meant that such elemental magic—literally "of the elements"—was part and parcel of a witches or wise woman's toolkit, and calling for rain upon a parched field one day could be a blessing as much as a storm at sea could be a curse.

As I write this, governments all around the world are beginning to announce a climate crisis, where extreme weather events have become dangerously common and solutions to the many complicated issues creating this issue are still thin on the ground. Weather magic alone will not be the

---

40. Spence, *Shetland Folk-lore*, location 688.

major factor in restoring some balance; we as humans need to take responsibility and practical steps to bring about change, but prayers to the spirits of our environment, especially at times of drought or deluge, can be surprisingly effective and restore a sense of co-creation and partnership with the natural world that has long term healing effects. Therefore, I ask that everyone performing weather magic take great care and forethought before any such undertaking. I stress that this sort of magic should only be used for the greater good, *not* to attempt to alter things for our own personal convenience; such selfish acts would ultimately endanger the practitioner and not engender the weather spirits' assistance. Good-intentioned and altruistic workings for the benefit of everyone are safe and may well make a difference in times of trouble.

☽ PRACTICAL ☾
TO CAPTURE THE WIND

On a gusty day, go to a high place and call upon your guides, allies, and especially your air spirit ally. Take with you a sturdy piece of thin *biodegradable* rope (never plastic or nylon) thick enough to easily untie later but thin enough to tie good knots into.

Call to the winds to aid your magic, and bow to each of the four airts, or directions. When you are ready, raise your rope up high until you feel a gust of wind upon you and through the rope. Tie a knot in the rope at one end, quickly and firmly. Call out "I bind you here, gentle wind! This is my will; it shall be done!"

With your arms still raised, remain holding the rope with both hands for another gust of wind. When you feel one, tie a second knot. Say, "I bind you here, better wind! This is my will; it shall be done!"

Once more, raise your arms and the rope to gather a third gust. Tie your final knot, saying. "I bind you here, fierce wind! This is my will; it shall be done, and harm none all three!"

When your third knot is tied, hold up the knotted rope and call to the winds. Tell them that these shall be undone only in need and harming none.[41]

Traditional Tales

To Untie the Wind (Outer Hebrides)

> A boatman from one of the southern islands was long detained in Lewis by adverse winds. He was courting a witch's daughter, and applied to her mother for a favourable wind. He gave her a pound of tobacco, and, assisted by neighbouring witches, after three days' exertion, she produced a string with three knots upon it. The first knot was called "Come Gently" (Thig gu fòill), and when he loosened it as he left the shore, a gentle breeze sprang up. The second knot was called "Come better" (Teann na's fhearr), and on its being untied the breeze came "Stiffen." As he neared the harbour, he loosened the last knot out of curiosity, the name of which was "Hardship" (Cruaidh-chàs). A wind came "to blow the hillocks out of their places" (sèideadh nan cnoc), which sent the thatch of the houses into the furrows of the plough-land, and the boatman was drowned. In Harris, they say the boat was drawn up on land and secured before the last knot was untied. She was capsized and smashed to pieces.[42]

This wonderful teaching tale shows us how great caution is needed when working with the winds, and when we undo the first knot we should be clear that we call out to the skies for a gentle wind, when we undo the second knot, we should call for a better wind, but we should never undo

---

41. This spell is by the author, based on a great many traditional versions found throughout the UK.

42. Campbell, *Witchcraft and Second Sight*, location 217.

Untie the Wind

the third knot, for its always said a great storm will blow at its undoing; instead, we should bury the rope when the first two are undone or place it in the sea, where one day when the third knot biodegrades, the wind can go free and do no harm.

☽ PRACTICAL ☾
SPELL TO RAISE THE WIND

This traditional spell to raise the wind is found in numerous variations across the UK; the words from this version are from the always-fascinating Isobel Gowdie, a witch from Auldearn in Scotland who lived in the seventeenth century.

Take a fully biodegradable cotton cloth—a damp or wet one if you would bring rain with the wind—and seek a standing stone or large boulder out upon the land. Call in your allies first for protection, and then beat the cloth upon the stone, over and over, reciting:

"I knock this rag upon this stone
To raise the wind in the devils (or *the old gods*) name*
It shall not lie till I please again!"[43]

Let yourself fall into a semi trance with this practice, feeling for yourself when to end. Keep the cloth and put it somewhere safe when you are done.

If you feel you need to end this spell, take the cloth back to the place with the boulder, and call out to the winds, "My spell is done, go now in peace and harm none!" and lay the cloth flat upon the boulder. Leave it there for an hour, and then bury it.

Note to reader: "The devil" as mentioned by Scottish witches of the sixteenth and seventeenth centuries was almost always interchangeable with the king or queen of the faeries—there is no need to call upon any "devil" here. Instead I call upon "the old gods," as I feel they and I know each other somewhat better.

☽ PRACTICAL ☾
SLOWING THE STORM

This traditional weather spell uses a hag or holey stone tied to a strong piece of string about four feet in length. Versions of this have been practiced in Cornwall especially (in addition to all over the Celtic diaspora), Sometimes, a bullroarer was used or another weighted string or rope instead. This version is my own.

Calling in your familiar spirits, stand at a high place. Call in the wind by spinning the rope clockwise, faster and faster in front of you like a spindle, or over your head like a slingshot. To decrease the wind and the power of the storm, spin the thread and the hag stone anticlockwise, slower and slower, calling all the time for the storm and the winds to slow and cease.

Prayers to the thunder god Taranis, whose symbol is the wheel, are also helpful for this task. It may be that the spinning hag stone or bullroarer

---

43. From "The confessions of Isobel Gowdie," Auldearne, Scotland, 1662. Reproduced in *Book of British Spells & Charms* (Troy Books, 2015), 253.

mimics the spinning movement of Taranis's wheel, and bullroarers have been found in Britain which may have been used for this purpose.

) PRACTICAL (
A SPELL TO CEASE THE RAIN

Sometimes old magic is retained in our cultural memory in the form of children's rhymes, and this is a good example. The second half is usually forgotten, however, and reveals an example of the old practice of making an offering to the weather spirits. Use this spell only when there is too much rain and there is a risk of flooding and danger.

Go out to the rain with the offering of a freshly baked cake, the best you can manage with your own hands made with the best ingredients you can afford.

Stand out in the open rain, and recite:

> "Rain, rain, go away, come again another day,
> And I will brew and I will bake
> And I will make you another cake!"

Lay the cake upon the ground, as an offering to the rain, bow and return the way you came, not looking back.

When the rain ceases, thank the skies, and when the rain returns, give them another fresh baked offering, just as you said you would. Don't ask them to go this time, instead, earn their trust and friendship by giving it freely. In time if you build a good relationship with the weather spirits, they are more and more likely to work with you for the higher good of all. This is a practice that takes time, but harms none and is more responsible given the environmental challenges of our present time.

Natural Navigation

It's really useful to own a compass and to take the time to notice the four directions where you live and what lays in the landscape on your horizons. With a little observation, however, you can learn to navigate your way through an area or know your four compass directions by observing signs in nature as well as solar, lunar, and stellar details.

The Path of the Sun, the Path of the Moon

Most people know that the sun rises in the east and sets in the west, but in fact the position of the sun at dawn and sunset and its path across the sky differs over the course of the year. At midwinter in the northern hemisphere, the sun rises in the southeast and sets in the south west, tracking across the sky in its most southerly position for the whole year, giving us the shorter days and colder temperatures. The opposite occurs for the summer solstice, when it rises in the northeast, its most northerly position, and sets in the northwest. The sun only tracks across the sky along the east-west axis twice a year during the spring and autumn equinoxes. At midday, the sun appears at its highest point in the sky but is directly affected by latitude and the date—highest in the midday sky in June, and lowest in late December. These positions can be measured using your hands; the December sun will rarely raise above two fists above the horizon, whereas the June sun it will rise nearer to six, depending on the size of your hands. Nothing beats personal observations of our landscapes to illustrate these things; once learnt, this is knowledge which is never lost.

It's also possible to make calculations using a simple sextant, which measures these angles more accurately.

☽ PRACTICAL ☾
MEASURING SHADOWS

Using a straight stick, place it in the ground vertically and measure its shadow, beginning in the morning and marking it on the ground over several hours. The shortest shadow each day will be a perfect north-south line, as the sun is due south when at its highest point in the sky. The length of the shadow is also variable over the year—longest at midwinter, shortest midsummer, and in March and September over the equinoxes, the same length.

Sunsets

It's possible to work out what time sunset will occur by holding up your fist again towards the sun: every knuckle the sun is above the horizon represents approximately a quarter of an hour of sunlight left, a little more further north, a little less further south. The sunset is longer and shallower further north, till it is horizontal at the north pole.

Moon Cycles

Generally rising in the northeast or southeast and setting in the northwest or southwest, the moon's cycle takes approximately twenty-eight days to complete. From the dark or new moon (where no moon is visible or only its thinnest crescent), through waxing crescent, to waxing gibbous (over a crescent but not full), to full, the moon then wanes, gradually thinning through waning gibbous, to crescent, to new or dark moon again.

The moon's cycle in relationship to the stars is more complex; in relation to the stars, observing the moon's position in the exact same position takes nineteen years. Known as the Metonic cycle, it was recorded in the alignments of numerous Neolithic stone circles and procession ways, as well as etched in the stones at Knowth in Ireland, dating from 3200 BCE, five thousand years ago.

It is possible to determine the compass points—north, south, east, and west—using the moon. Unless the moon is full, this method works quite well to determine which direction is south, which in turn allows you to discern the other directions. Wherever it is in the sky, use the two endpoints of the crescent to point you towards the horizon. Follow this line down to the earth, where it falls will be approximately south. When it reaches its highest point in the sky before it has begun to descend again, when still moving left to right but not up or down, you'll again be looking south. The lower the moon nears the horizon, the rougher and less accurate this becomes, but it works as a guide in many circumstances. It may also help to mark its shadows.

Full moons rise roughly opposite the direction of sunset on that day—around midsummer, they rise well north of east, and around midwinter towards the south east. They also rise at the same time as the sunset. A younger waxing moon will rise earlier than sunset, and a waning moon will rise later. A new moon rises at the same time as the sun so is invisible, but rises fifty minutes later ever day, till the full moon equates to the time of sunset, and then fifty minutes later and later till it is in time for the sunrise again. Useful to know when planning night time walks and moon magic!

Star Lore: The Main Constellations (Northern Hemisphere)

The Iron Age druids were known to study the stars, likely knowledge that was handed down over generations. Detailed stellar observations take time and skill, but across Britain and Ireland are megalithic sites dating from the Neolithic and the Bronze ages which were astronomically aligned. Items such as the Coligny calendar of the second century CE show that this sophisticated knowledge continued into the Iron Age and Romano-Celtic periods. While most of the star lore of the druids is now lost, none the less, colloquial names for the stars and the constellations continued in Celtic cultures, and these may well retain some traces of what was lost.

To cover all the constellations would be beyond the remit of this book, but knowing a few of them can help you discern your directions and add a deeper level to your awareness and your practice. There are tons of books, star maps, computer programs, and apps to help you with mapping and exploring the stars, but the major ones are listed here to help you get started.

Ursa Major—The Big Bear, the Plough, Arthur's Wain

Also known as the Big Dipper, Ursa Major is a collection of four stars in a loose square with a tail, so it looks like a spoon, dipper, or like its old name Arthurs Wain, Arthurs plough. This is perhaps the most famous and easily spotted constellation. It is found roughly towards the north.

Polaris—The North Star

To find Polaris, draw an invisible line in your mind from the two stars at the front of the big dipper/ plough, straight on up and to the right—the next bright star is Polaris, and it always points to true north.

Ursa Minor—The Little Bear

To be sure you've found Polaris, it's helpful to be aware that Polaris itself is the tail end or last star in the handle of the little dipper, Ursa Minor, the little bear. This constellation looks just like the big dipper but is smaller and upside down, appearing above it.

Corona Borealis—Caer Arianrhod

The Corona Borealis, or the northern crown, is known in Welsh lore as Caer Arianrhod, the castle of Arianrhod. Arianrhod (whose name means *silver wheel*) appears in the fourth branch of the Mabinogi, a collection of Welsh myths. Corona Borealis is a neat semi-circle of stars once again appearing in the north. One of the easiest ways is to look out for the bright Vega, a brilliant blue star in the northeast. To the west of it is another bright star, Arcturus, which is orange, and can be found by following the arc of the big dippers handle downwards. If you draw a line between Vega and Arcturus, it will travel first through the figure of Hercules, then through Corona Borealis.

Cassiopeia—Llys Dôn, the Court of the Welsh Mother Goddess Dôn

Another constellation in the north sky, Cassiopeia, looks like the letter W or an M, depending where it is in its arc across the sky. Once you have located Polaris, it can be found by going down and to the left.

Orion the Hunter—Gwyn ap Nudd

Orion appears below the horizon during the summer months but is found easily in the southern sky over the autumn and winter. Gwyn ap Nudd is known in Welsh lore as the ruler of Annwfn, the otherworld, as well as a king of the faeries. To find this huge constellation first look for the diagonal line of three stars known as Orion's belt. Orion is accompanied by Sirius, the dog star, which lies below him to the left and is part of the constellation Canis Major, the big dog.

Heliacal Rising Stars

An important astronomical event to many of our Celtic and earlier ancestors was the heliacal rising of certain stars. Due to the earth's movement around the sun, some stars are not visible to us year-round. Certain stars have traditionally held great importance to the agricultural and spiritual traditions all around the world, and their disappearance and return marked important yearly cycles. A heliacal rising is the return of one of these important stars after a period of absence, where it is observed rising above the horizon just before dawn. This appearance is its first moment of return, as the star becomes visible for a short period before the sun makes it invisible until the next dawn, when it will be seen for slightly longer, and so on.

Vervain and the Dog Star

One of the most important heliacal rising stars in the Celtic tradition is the dog star, Sirius, part of the constellation Canis Major. It's the brightest star in the night sky and was highly important to Iron Age druids. Vervain, one of the most sacred plants in the Celtic tradition was gathered when Sirius rose so the plant was not touched by the light of the sun or moon when it was harvested. This could occur on a night with no visible moon or when it is cloudy for the best effects. These gathering conditions may not have been possible every year, so it's possible it was only gathered occasionally, or there was a bit of flexibility here. First the earth was given a gift of honey in thanks, and a circle was drawn around the plant with an iron blade, before being pulled up with the left hand and held up to Sirius to be imbued with its first rays upon the earth.[44] This simple, ancient ritual is easily performed

---

44. Pliny, *Historia Naturalis*, Book 25, 59, 2. Translated by John Bostock, (London: Taylor and Francis, Red Lion Court, Fleet Street. 1855.) http://www.perseus.tufts.edu/hopper/text?doc=Perseus%3Atext%3A1999.02.0137%3Abook%3D25%3Achapter%3D59.

today and lends an extra magic to the herbal uses for the plant as well as deeper insight into the plants unique energies.

To calculate when Sirius will rise at your location, you must first know your latitude (numerous websites can help) but for a rough guide, it will rise between mid-July to mid-August, approximately 45 minutes before sunrise, facing south. According to the Old Farmer's Almanac, the traditional "dog days" of summer last for forty days from July 3 to August 11, but this will vary depending on your location.

Five

FIRE

After exploring the sacred Celtic triplicity of earth, sea, and sky, we turn our attention now to fire, that other element. In many ways, fire lies at the heart of many spiritual practices in the Celtic traditions.

Fire Magic

To the Celts, fire has always been of central importance. Whether it be the hearth fire—the heart of the home—or the *teine-eigin*, the need fire lit at the fire festivals of Beltane and Samhain to bless the community and the live-stock, fire has always been seen as life-giving, cleansing, and protecting. As such, a host of traditional lore and practices are attached to it. Every early community around the world has honoured the importance of fire, and seen it as a magical tool, central to life in every way, bringing light and heat. This continued in Britain and Ireland well into the early twentieth century, when homes were still heated by open fires. Today its elemental presence is being sought out once more, and wood-burners have become fashionable in many British homes, bringing back a sensuality and living energy that has been sorely missed in most centrally heated buildings. In the Celtic worldview, every home must have a hearth fire as both a central energetic point in the

121

house and also for the spirits and ancestors. There are many tales told of faeries of the hearth, and British and Irish folk magic attest to the many spells and protective charms placed upon a fire or up in the chimney to protect from malicious spirits ranging from witch bottles containing protective magical items to mummified cats and children's shoes. Equally, fires outside on the land were the heart of community celebrations, and the comfort of every traveller or hunter in the wild northern landscape, a place of storytelling and magic, ease and security that held the dark at bay. The protective magic of the fire is ancient and powerful. The ability to light your own fires from nothing is both an essential practical skill for anyone who spends time outdoors, as well as its own deep magic that will assist you in your own wild magic.

Ways to Connect with the Fire Spirits

Learn to light safe fires. Have evenings of only candlelight. Try a fire walk. Learn fire-poi. Dance. Cook on an open fire. Barbeque. Write down your worries and burn them on a bonfire. Contemplate the sun and the earth's fiery heart.

Beltane and Samhain fires

Traditionally, especially in Scotland and Ireland, Beltane ("the fires of the god Bel," May1/5) and Samhain ("summer's end"—October 31/November 7) are the two main Celtic fire festivals, the others being Imbolc (February 2) and Lughnasadh (August 1). At Beltane and Samhain, all the fires in the community were extinguished, and would be re-lit from a central fire. In the Irish Cormac's Glossary, we see that two fires would be lit, and the cattle and any sick persons would go between these two fires to drive out sickness and other negative energies such as bad fortune or ill wishes. The same twin fires were used in Scotland, to bring healing and good luck giving rise to the Gaelic proverbial saying: *eadar dà theine Bhealltuinn* ("between two Beltane fires").

> The inhabitants here did also make use of a fire called *tin-egin*, i.e., a forced fire, or fire of necessity, which they used as an antidote against the plague or murrain in cattle; and it was performed thus: all the fires in the parish were extinguished,

and then eighty-one married men, being thought the necessary number for effecting this design, took two great planks
of wood, and nine of them were employed by turns, who
by their repeated efforts rubbed one of the planks against
the other until the heat thereof produced fire; and from this
forced fire each family is supplied with new fire, which is no
sooner kindled than a pot full of water is quickly set on it,
and afterwards sprinkled upon the people infected with the
plague, or upon the cattle that have the murrain.[45]

M. Martin, *A Description of the*
Western Islands of Scotland, 1703

Celtic Fire Churn as per Description Below

This incredible imagery describes a community sized fire lighting technique, known as a Celtic fire-churn, taking place in the early eighteenth
century. There are many ways of lighting a fire without matches or a
lighter, and this one is similar to a technique known today as the bow drill
method, only on a massive scale. While using so many people is not to my

45. Martin, *Western Islands of Scotland*, 1229–1231.

knowledge practiced today, smaller scale fire churns are still made, although more often for the use of one or two people at a time and can be a very effective way of creating fire. Something similar is done in Russia where it is known as a fire-door, which suits it well: the fire is made underneath a doorframe-shaped structure of two vertical planks with a cross beam, and the central fire drill turned by ropes in the middle. Calling it a door is a wonderful way of imagining the fire as coming from spirit through it to manifest in this world.

Blessing of the Kindling

Every household naturally would have its own fire, as many do still to this day, and blessing the fire was traditionally performed daily (if not twice a day) not only to keep the fire lit, but also to keep the house safe from an out of control fire, as the possible danger from open hearths was immense. Every hearth functioned as the heart of the home, and this revolved around the careful relationship between the family and this powerful presence in their midst. For this reason, in Ireland and Scotland especially, the hearth was usually placed under the protection of the fire goddess Brighid, who later became Saint Brigit, called upon each day to place her care over hearth and home.

This blessing was traditionally performed by the woman of the house, who would say the following prayer or one like it as she stirred the hearth fire back to life first thing in the morning. Traditionally the prayer would be spoken softly, breathed into the hearth rather than proclaimed loudly due to its role in the hearth-keepers relationship with the fire, a private relationship and private, even solemn daily ritual.

The following kindling prayer, which calls upon Saint Brigid, is from the Outer Hebrides in Scotland and was still in use in 1900 and beyond. It's an example of the practice of syncretism, a common feature in Celtic communities where the old Pagan ways and Christianity blended more or less seamlessly. As such, it's perfectly permissible to make your own or adapt this one to have a more Pagan flavour; it can be used for outdoor fires just as well as for hearth fires:

Kindling Prayer

TOGAIDH mis an tula
Mar a thogadh Muire.
Cairn Bhride 's Mhuire
Air an tula 's air an lar,
'S air an fhardaich uile.

Co iad ri luim an lair?
Eoin, Peadail agus Pail.
Co iad ri bruaich mo leap?
Bride bhuidheach 's a Dalt.
Co iad ri fath mo shuain?
Muire ghraidh-gheal 's a h-Uan.
Co siud a tha 'n am theann?
Righ na grein e fein a th' ann,
Co siud ri cul mo chinn?
Mac nan dul gun tus, gun linn.

I WILL raise the hearth-fire
As Mary would.
The encirclement of Bride and of Mary
On the fire, and on the floor,
And on the household all.

Who are they on the bare floor?
John and Peter and Paul.
Who are they by my bed?
The lovely Bride and her Fosterling.
Who are those watching over my sleep?
The fair loving Mary and her Lamb.
Who is that a-near me?
The King of the sun, He himself it is.
Who is that at the back of my head?
The Son of Life without beginning, without time.[46]

---

46. Carmichael, *Carmina Gadelica, Volume I*, 83.

Smooring the Fire

Smooring, (*smàladh* in Scots Gaelic) essentially means subduing or smothering as a way of ritually settling a fire down for the night.

Though less environmentally friendly than many other options available today, peat is still the traditional fuel for many in Scotland and Ireland. Peat burns hot but with less flame and light. However, it has slow long-burning embers; settling it down for the night to be revived in the morning works well. A similar approach can be taken with a wood fire, but more care must be taken for safety and effectiveness—so long as a fire guard is in place, or if outdoors, nothing flammable is placed too close by.

The smooring ritual is done with great gentle care and can be a thing of great beauty. The embers are spread evenly across the hearth and shaped into a circle. The circle is then divided into three equal parts with space between them all. Then a peat, or a chunk of peat is laid down between each of the three sections. Smaller wood logs are also suitable for this purpose. Traditionally, during Christian times, the first was laid down in the name of the god of life, the second in the name of the god of peace, and the third in the name of the god of grace. This could easily be changed to honour the Three Mothers, the Dea Matronae, or each in the name of Brighid, the god Bel, or any other of your choice. Equally, a prayer for other things such as protection, guidance, and healing could accompany each peat or log, laying them down in the name of life, peace, and grace is sufficient. The remaining ash is then heaped over the peats and the embers to bank it down effectively for the night.

A Traditional Highland Scottish Smooring Prayer

> AN Tri numh
> A chumhnadh,
> A chomhnadh,
> A chomraig
> An tula,
> An taighe,
> An teaghlaich,
> An oidhche,

An nochd,
O! an oidhche,
An nochd,
Agus gach oidhche,
Gach aon oidhche.
Amen.

THE sacred Three
To save,
To shield,
To surround
The hearth,
The house,
The household,
This eve,
This night,
Oh! this eve,
This night,
And every night,
Each single night.
Amen.[47]

Fire Lighting Methods

Basic fire lighting

Preparation

To light a basic fire anywhere—in the hearth at home or in nature—you first need to prepare your ground. First consider the position of your fire. Out in the wild, you will need to know you have permission when necessary and that there are no overhanging tree branches that may catch—remember that the space directly above a fire is hotter than you may think! Clear the area of ash if it has been used before. If in nature, be especially careful to clear away any dried leaves and twigs and that no small animals could be

---

47. Carmichael, *Carmina Gadelica*, Volume 1, 84.

affected. You also need to make sure the ground is not excessively dry—it is possible for a wildfire to start when roots are burned underground, so take heed of any fire exclusion zones. When in doubt, use a fire bowl.

Next, gather your tinder, kindling, and larger pieces of fuel. Ensure that all materials are dry and ready yet a sensible distance from your intended fire so that they cannot accidentally catch.

Fire-lighting happens in three stages:

1. Tinder: To take the spark to a flame, or to light with a flame from matches/lighter.

2. Kindling : To take the flame into a small fire.

3. Wood/fuel: Once the small fire is going, the flames will be large and hot enough to ignite smaller logs, after which increasingly larger logs may be added for a more sustained burn.

Tinder: Tinder is a fine-textured combustible material that will ignite with a small spark. When this is burning, slightly larger material can be added, increasing in size from twigs to logs until the fire is fully burning. In a hearth, tinder may be tight balls of newspaper, or firelighters that can be lit with a match. Outdoors, tinder can be several things you can bring with you such as charcloth, cotton wool balls, or jute twine. You may also use fully natural materials such as dry birch bark, cattail fluff, usnea lichen, and some varieties of dried fungi, such as cramp ball fungus (*Daldinia concentrica*), also known as king Alfred's cakes in the UK which is a round, knobby-shaped fungus that grows on ash trees. Tinder can also be made by using a stick and a knife. Cut away any bark to get to the drier heartwood. Drawing the knife away from you down the length, cut thin curls of wood; this is sometimes called a *feather stick*.

Kindling: Kindling is larger and made of more dense materials than tinder; small, dry twigs or thin slivers of split logs are ideal for this. Add them one at a time until you have a small, steady fire with a few small burning wood coals underneath. You may need more kindling than you think, so gather plenty.

Fuel: Wood needs to be dry to burn. There are advanced techniques for lighting a fire in wet conditions, but you'll first need to be proficient in other fire-lighting techniques before any attempts.

Seasoned logs: Wood that has been left outside for at least a season if not a year—are best to burn. It's ideal if it has been cut into logs just after felling and the bark is left on. The less moisture in the wood, the hotter and cleaner the burn with less smoke. And if you are using wood-burner, your chimney or glass burner doors will be cleaner. That said, getting seasoned wood in the wild will mean bringing it with you or seeking dry fallen wood in your area. With a little practice and care, it is possible to chop branches into smaller logs or to place a longer branch over the fire at one end and gently and gradually feed it in over time.

If you're not experienced with using an axe, a small hand axe will be adequate for cutting most logs in the wild off fallen branches. Small folding saws are sometimes easier (and a little safer), and wire saws are super light but take some muscle to use on all but the thinnest branches. All these tools are relatively cheap; don't go for whatever's cheapest but instead tools that are higher quality. Higher quality tools last longer and are very light and portable … perfect for the hedge druid's or wild witch's backpack!

Making Your Spark

It is perfectly possible to light a fire for magical or spiritual purposes using matches or a lighter with fire-lighting blocks before adding the kindling. I've seen many indigenous shamans from around the world use fuel of this kind, and the results have still been powerful and sacred. However, I feel it's best to use traditional fire-lighting techniques if you can. Firstly, these are skills our ancestors would have taken for granted, and to continue learning their skills is itself a living prayer of honour. Secondly, starting fires in this way forms a much deeper and more powerful offering to the spirits, our ancestors, and the spirits of the fire and fuel. When using the old methods, we are creating a physical manifestation of the pure forms of the fire spirit we are calling in. It's also deeply satisfying!

Fire–steel

One of the easiest ways to light a magical fire from scratch (not using a lighter/matches and firelighters) is to use a fire steel, also known as a magnesium fire stick. These are relatively modern inventions but are an improved, more efficient design based on the use of flint and steel, or a knife and fire striker (more on those later). Fire-steel is basically a steel rod coated in a cerium and iron alloy, and a steel scraper. When the surface of this rod is scraped at speed, it gives off very hot sparks which can ignite your tinder. These molten sparks are VERY hot, producing temperatures of around 3000°C (5500°F) but are really easy to use and relatively safe—the sparks go out very quickly unless they catch on some tinder. They are reliable and unlike matches or a lighter, work fine if they've got wet—all they need is a quick wipe to dry. A single fire steel is also ultra-portable and can be used thousands of times. The rod is usually given a black coating to prevent rusting, which requires you to strike it hard enough to scrape to get your spark, but it's easier than it sounds.

You will first need to prepare the area where you are lighting your fire and gather your tinder, kindling, and fuel. Wispy and fluffy tinder works best with a fire-steel.

Gather a small pile of tinder with a slightly larger layer of kindling beneath it. Have your tinder and kindling close together so that the flame can spread, but don't make your pile/layer of kindling so dense air cannot travel around it. As with all outdoor fires, light yours in a relatively sheltered spot out of strong wind.

Hold your fire-steel diagonally downwards just above the tinder. Kneel carefully before your intended fire at a close distance over it but not so close that you risk burning yourself. Be calm and steady, fire lighting takes patience and care. Be sensible and present in what you are doing, anticipating what's likely to happen next.

Strike down the fire-steel with the scraper, away and downwards from you, close to or over the tinder. Start by holding the scraper at an angle of about 90-100 degrees to the rod, about halfway or two-thirds up the rod. Your strike needs to be relatively fast (but not super-fast), and quite firm. Don't go up and down the fire-steel, only strike downwards and away from you. Some people find it easier to reverse the tools and drag the fire-steel down firmly over the scraper, but the motion is the same. It can take a few goes to get the knack; be patient, and practice before you ever need to light a fire in the wild for any warmth or survival reasons. It is simple to do but is something you learn by muscle memory and experience rather than logically; don't presume just by reading this you can light a fire at need without trying in more relaxed circumstances first!

When the sparks hit the tinder, be very gentle but quick to add more tinder if necessary. Then add the smallest grade of kindling, gradually adding more (you'll need to add this fairly quickly, but not so fast as to smother the flame.) Let the flame get strong enough first. When you've a nice pile of kindling burning, you may then begin adding your fuel—larger logs or peat bricks. (And once again remember that while the use of peat is traditional, it is not environmentally sound!)

After you've become proficient at using a fire-steel with its intended scraper, you might like to try using a knife with the fire-steel rod. The technique is basically the same but take care to strike *away* from you... especially when a blade is involved! Most bushcraft knives work for this purpose, but these days you can easily find good knives with a special fire lighting part on the back edge of the blade. Fire-steel rods of varying sizes can also be bought on their own for use like this, or for replacing your kit when the rod has run out of strikes, which will happen over a long period of use.

Flint and Steel

This is my favourite method of fire lighting, as it has that ancient, ancestral feel to it; care and skill must be used to make it successful, yet it is also relatively quick and with practice is as reliable as a modern fire-steel.

This method requires sharp-edged flint flakes that are fairly robust and large enough (about half to a third the size of your hand) to hold steadily with your hands at a safe distance from where you are striking to avoid scratched or nicked fingers with a fine sharp edge. You also need a fire striker—these are in all sorts of shapes but are usually a variation on a

D-shape with a rounded side to hold with your fingers and a straight edge to strike the flint with. By striking the flint with the steel, you get a smaller and duller spark than with fire-steel, and you need some especially fine tinder to spark to a flame. Charcloth is excellent for this (you can make it yourself or buy it online), or you could use a fungus like the cramp ball fungus discussed earlier. If you use charcloth, place it with some fine tinder underneath it, such as jute threads (pulled from jute twine), and lain already in a small bed of fibrous birch bark, dry straw, grass, or cotton wool. Have other gradually larger materials to hand at guide the spark to a flame and to a fire from this point.

Holding the flint in one hand, strike the steel against it, close and directly over your charcloth. You might like to try holding the charcloth underneath the flint with its edge poking out slightly to catch the spark this way. Hold the flint horizontally and strike the steel upon it at a 90-degree angle. This takes a fair bit of practice; you need to do it with quick and short but quite firm strokes. Try doing it in a three-fold rhythm—*tap tap-tap! Tap tap-tap!* I find this often works best for me; the best spark usually happens on the third tap, but one tap is enough for the more experienced. The trick is all in the firmness and confidence of your strike, the angle, and in the edge of your flint—too dull and it won't spark, too fine and it'll break off without effect. Again, using this tool becomes easier with experience but can be done with just common sense when the materials are at hand. There is no easy way around it—using steel and flint takes practice, practice, and more practice, but once you've got it, you'll find it will come easier next time.

When you have your spark, you need to support it growing into an ember immediately by placing it in the finest grade tinder you have—a nest of very fine birch bark, horse hoof fungus shavings, or jute threads all work well—which is in turn laid on a football-sized bed of dry grass or straw. You can then fold the straw over your ember and gently lift and blow into it (sometimes just a small wave of your straw bundle is enough) and it will suddenly catch into flame. The moment when it suddenly ignites and you have a ball of fire in your hand, with the straw burning upwards is wonderful and lots of fun. At this stage you can lay it down again into your bed of more tinder and kindling, adding fuel when it is well enough established.

Flint and Iron Pyrite Balls

You can use the same method for flint and steel with flint and chunks of naturally sourced iron pyrite—flint and iron pyrite occur close together in nature so were often found by our ancestors in the same vicinity. The iron pyrite chunks do not have a sharp edge, so you will have to strike the flint off of them rather than the other way around. Catch the spark immediately by striking them together over a prepared nest of tinder (horse hoof fungus or birch bark shavings work best for this) before moving onto larger tinder and then kindling.

Bow-drill Method

Lighting a fire using a bow drill is one of the simplest yet widely used techniques among indigenous peoples, with subtle variations in form. Keep in mind that this method does take time, skill, and hard work. Bow-drill methods are thought to date back to the Palaeolithic Era, and it is possible to use this technique with equipment made from scratch using nothing but a knife. The idea is that the bow has a string twisted around a wooden stick, the drill, which when rapidly pulled back and forth, spins against the hearth board to produce an ember.

Basic parts of the bow-drill method:

- Bow and string/cordage
- Hearth board
- Handhold block
- Drill
- Grease (optional)
- Various grades of tinder from the very fine to smaller twigs (previously prepared), larger sticks for fuel also on standby.

Making the bow-drill: A bow-drill is made by twisting the string from the bow to spin the drill which is held vertically between the hearth board and the handhold block. The handhold, or baring block is held in the other hand. Pressure is applied downwards to keep the drill spinning into the hearth board. The whole apparatus is held steady by placing your foot on the edge of the hearth board as you run the bow back and forwards quickly and repeatedly. The hearth board has a small notch cut into it at the site of the bow drill's friction; a heated black dust will form which will eventually ignite into a smoking ember. This ember needs to be quickly placed into a ball of tinder and blown gently but consistently until the tinder ignites. Be warned—this can take time!

Using the right kinds of wood is important for this type of fire lighting:

For the drill: Willow or hazel are the best, spruce or ash in second place.

For the hearth board: Willow or lime preferable; poplar, spruce, pine, and alder also work.

Experiment with different combinations that can easily be sourced in your surroundings, and notice the effects of the different seasons, as well as the condition of the wood. The ideal wood for the bow-drill is neither too dense, hard, nor too soft. Try sticking your thumbnail into the grain to feel it for yourself.

Making the Hearth Board

Find a suitable piece of wood from which to carve the board. As stated above, this wood must be dry and dead; the fallen wood commonly found on the forest floor is usually damp or has some rot. Look instead for dead standing trees, or an already seasoned piece, and try to select pieces which do not have knots. If you must cut, the piece you need must be about a foot long, four inches wide, and at least twice as wide as the thickness of your intended drill. Using a large knife, hatchet, or hand axe, carefully cut the piece so that it resembles a small flat plank, cut along the grain. Cut the piece to be about an inch thick.

The Drill

The drill or spindle needs to be about a foot long, and straight vertically grained; a split piece from your board works well. The same requirements for the wood apply—dry and seasoned. Trim this piece to be slightly less than an inch in diameter (e.g., the width of your thumb) and shape either end into sharp points. The drill doesn't have to be perfectly smooth, but fairly round with nothing to catch the string when you use the bow.

The Handhold Block

The handhold is a block of wood with which you press downwards onto the spindle. Cut it with a saw to roughly four or five inches square, about one or two inches thick with a flat base and top. Whittle and perhaps sand it top and bottom so that the spindle can sit in it and it is comfortable for your hand to grip and apply the pressure over several minutes. I've found using a thick cloth or a piece of leather rag can help; I've fairly small women's hands and need to be comfortable enough to apply the strength, and no one wants splinters or blisters! Gouge a small hole in the bottom big enough to house the pointed tip of the spindle, but not so deeply that it inhibits the turning. A smallish cone-shaped depression is ideal.

The Bow

Select a green, fresh branch (hazel and willow are good woods for this) as thick as your index finger and the length of your arm elbow to fingertip. It needs to be straight or have a slight bowlike curve and be springy but not weak. If the branch feels too stiff, whittling a little from the inside of the curve can help. Check to see that it bends evenly. Split each end vertically about two inches for the string.

The String

The string can be made out of all sorts of things—jute, leather, rawhide, cotton, and several types of cordage from wild plants such as nettle cordage, for example. Ropes made of nylon and plastic are okay but can melt from the friction. And in an emergency, you can even use shoelaces, although it needs to be pretty thick, around a quarter of an inch. Whatever you choose, string will fray from usage, but a quarter of an inch's thickness should last long enough for plenty of fire-starting over a year or so. Cut it to one and a half times the length of the bow. Using the splits at either end of your bow, tie it tightly using square or other knots such as the clove hitch that will catch and not undo. There are plenty of sources for knot-tying online, but the main idea is that you want it to be unpickable until you have it as taut as you want along the bow. Draw the string tight but not archery tight. When finished, the string should wrap around the spindle and tighten, ready for use.

Technique

With everything ready for your fire already prepared—space cleared, tinder, kindling, and fuel gathered, kneel with one foot on the edge of the hearth board: left foot if you are right-handed, so the board is on the inside of your foot and your other knee is to the right. Position the spindle about an inch from the edge and at the other end of the board so there is room. Pushing down with the block, let the spindle mark its position on the board. Next use a knife to scoop out a small funnel shape on this position to support the spindle tip. Wrap the string around the spindle so that it stands out-side the bow with one loop of cord around to make the cord very tight. Some adjustments might be necessary, but once you've tried it, it becomes common sense and straightforward. Position the bow in its notch and begin stroking the bow back and forth, to form the handhold hole and the hearth board hole enough to settle. If needed, use the knife again to adjust the holes so they fit better. When the holes are the right size, use some grease to lubricate the top of the spindle in the handhold if you have any. That way, most of your energy will be expended in creating the friction at the bottom.

Now cut a small notch next to your hearth board hole so that air can get into the hole. Place a small piece of wood or bark underneath to catch any smouldering coal.

Bow Drill

You are ready to start. Place the spindle in the notch with the cord twisted tight around it and move back and forth, pressing down with the handhold and bowing slightly downwards away from you and upwards towards you. Try to keep your back straight. Use the whole length of the string firmly and at a steady speed but not too quickly. Keep going! Gradually you will get some smoke—carefully lift the spindle to check. If it still smokes, you may have a coal. Use a twig or the tip of a knife and gently edge it out through the notch onto the wood you've laid to catch it and place it into a nest of tinder. There may be some more powder in the hearth-board hole which can be added to help keep it going. Bunch the tinder around the coal and gently blow on it, and it will catch. You'll need to lay it on its laid bed of more tinder and kindling straight away, before adding some fuel when it's fully established.

This technique takes practice and patience, and is the basic one-person form of what ancient Celtic communities used to light their community and ritual fires, now known as the Celtic Churn.

Celtic Churn

An incredible sight, the fire churn takes time, materials, and several people to prepare. There are numerous variations possible with this design, but essentially the technique is the same as a bow drill but on a larger scale. The drill is usually a straight sapling sized tree trunk of about 6 to 7 feet in height held in place by two vertical v-split tree trunks or forked branches secured in the ground, with a third crossbeam between them to provide the downwards pressure. A wooden board or pan is placed on the ground beneath the drill, which is tied round with rope, and pulled either by two groups of men on either side, or by one man, holding both ends of the rope, and pulling backwards and forwards. Records suggest whole grown oak trees were once used for this technique, and entire villages of men took part, which would have been an awe-inspiring sight.

Fire Laying Ceremony, Fire Offerings

There is little to no surviving lore on the practice of giving a sacred fire an offering in the Celtic tradition. The Romans did write dubious accounts concerning the practice of the Wicker Man, burning men and livestock in a vast wicker construction, but in practice this would prove highly imprac- tical, as wicker burns fast and relatively coolly, extinguishing long before an offering would be burnt. However, the practice of giving offerings to spirits generally is well attested, and it is something that is still widely practiced elsewhere, in shamanistic and animistic traditions around the world. Given that there is a host of lore in the Celtic regions concerning fire spirits and honouring the hearth spirits with offerings, it is likely that offerings to the fire itself in outdoor settings were practised at some time, in some form, and certainly taking up the practice now can deepen your relationship to the fire spirits with great effect.

Following the patterns of fire laying known from Celtic traditions such as smooring the fire, we can work with the idea of honouring the sacred three—earth, sea, and sky, the Celtic "three mothers," or the three faces of Brighid when lighting a fire. In this way when the area for fire lighting has been suitably and safely prepared, we can build our fire in a triskele pattern in three sections. Lay a bed of three suitable sticks rather like the letter *Y* or the peace sign, laying these first three sticks down as a base for the fire, taking a moment with each stick to thank the tree spirits, and the tree that it was a part of. Telling the fire-to-be that we give thanks to it also, we can then lay the first one down, in honour of the element of earth and all its abundance. Try these words or speak your own as you feel guided.

> Spirit of wood, spirit of this tree that was, I give thanks to you for your gift of fuel. Spirit of fire that will be, I give thanks to you and ask that you receive these gifts in friendship and honour. I lay this down in honour of wood, and fire, and the spirit of earth that holds us all!

Repeat with the next piece, repeating the same format, but this time finally in honour of the sea:

> Spirit of wood, spirit of tree that was, I give thanks to you for your gift of fuel. Spirit of fire that will be, I give thanks to you and ask that you receive these gifts in friendship and honour. I lay this down in honour of wood, and fire, and the spirit of sea that surrounds us all!

And finally, the sky:

> Spirit of wood, spirit of tree that was, I give thanks to you for your gift of fuel. Spirit of fire that will be, I give thanks to you and ask that you receive these gifts in friendship and honour. I lay this down in honour of wood, and fire, and the spirit of sky that breathes us all!

Next, make an offering to these three sticks and the circle of the fire itself, either by placing a small pile of herbs, honey, or cream in each of the three sections, or by gently and carefully making a circle of herbs around the edge and along the three "spokes."

Some suitable herbs are mugwort, meadowsweet, roses, vervain, or juniper, although the type of herbal offering could suit the purpose of the fire or the season.

Offerings of cream or honey work well, as does a freshly baked bannock, broken into three pieces, one for each section.

When making the offering, start with giving thanks for the offering itself: the plant, the bees that made the honey, the bread that made the bannock, and so on. Then speak to the fire-to-be and the surrounding spirits. Ask them to receive this offering given in friendship. Try these words or, again, use your own:

> Spirit of the mugwort, I thank you for your friendship and
> your support, I give you now to the spirits of this fire, that
> you may be transformed, and inspire my visions. Spirits of the
> fire that will be, accept my offering as a sign of my friendship
> and respect.

You can then lay a bed of kindling again following the triskele pattern. Make sure you have your finer kindling materials close by to take the spark or the char and get the fire going.

I find making a sacred fire is a ritual in and of itself, and one that needs time and careful preparation, where every aspect of the fire is thought out carefully, from safety considerations and practicalities such as having all your materials at hand before you begin, to the magical and spiritual matters such as your prayers and offerings, and indeed the purpose of the fire itself.

Fire Divination

With time and practice, fire divination and scrying can serve as a deep and insightful dialogue between you and the fire spirits. There are many tra-

ditional Celtic fire divination techniques that stem from this initial awareness of the fire spirit and the lighting of a ritual fire. In times past, even the
home's hearth fire would have been lit from a ritual flame and honoured
as sacred, as discussed earlier. The play of flames and shadows upon the
wall or the patterns in the ash in the morning could have been considered
omens of many things.

It was once a regular practice to burn the straw mattress of someone
when they died—and the ash from this was especially ominous—with those
present looking out for a footprint in the ashes that might match one of
those present. Such a footprint was said to identify the person who would
die next. Burning mattresses no longer happens even in rural communities,
but the fire from a traditional wake or funeral gathering can also be used to
seek omens and signs- not for who might die next- but for messages from
those who have passed, or other guidance from the spirit world, at a time
when the powers of fate and mortality feel particularly strong.

The fire was seen as both a home's heart and spirit; and any unexpected
activity or sign around the hearth was always noted as communication
from the spirit of the fire or the household spirits in some form. In Shetland, a whole system of reading the fire formed around the movements of
the flames and the fuel as it burnt.

> A brand standing by itself in the fire was called a guest; a smok-
> ing brand betokened an unwelcome guest, while a bright brand
> meant a friend. The coming of the unwelcome guest might be
> prevented by pouring water on the brand, but care was needed
> lest the act should bring misfortune on a friend, who might fall
> into a mire or burn.[48]

Fire Scrying

Using fire for scrying is relatively simple but takes time, and the practice
suits some temperaments better than others. Scrying of this kind works
best in a fire that has been ritually laid, lit, and honoured as a living spirit,

---

48. Spence, *Shetland Folk-lore*, 1697.

which can be done in many ways. Acknowledge the fire spirit as an ally and friend and make it an offering; a fragrant or magically relevant herb is the most common. Speak to it in your own words or try these to get yourself started:

> Spirit of the fire, bright one, I thank you for your warmth and illumination—show me what I need to know, blessed one.

Good herbs to offer the fire are mugwort or juniper, or a handful of incense. Gently and carefully cast the herbs into the fire saying,

> Accept these gifts, friend…

Settle down to sit by the fire, getting yourself comfortable and calmly present. Let your eyes rest upon the flames and embers, and see what you will see. It may take several hours, and is often best performed late at night, when the mood—both your own and that of the environment around you—feels conducive to such work. You may from time to time ask the fire questions politely and with gratitude. Let the flames' movements form a kind of body language and gesture you can feel as a response. Divination of this kind is more of an art form and is dependent on a shift in consciousness, so look for feelings and symbolism for your answers rather than yes or no responses.

Fire Cleansing

The traditional Beltane fires were lit for cleansing and blessing- cattle were often driven between two large Beltane fires to cleanse them of illness and pests, as well as ill wishes and attacks by unfriendly spirits. In the same way, fire can be used for energetic cleansing and blessing today. It all comes down to the purpose and practicalities of what you are looking to cleanse and why. A ritually lit fire can be used to cleanse and bless magical tools: hold them over the flames or waft them through the smoke. Equally, a home or a person can be cleansed by taking a fire brand from your ritual fire and circling the home or person anticlockwise to rid the home of ill will, misfortune, or unwelcome spirits; and clockwise to bring in blessings, protection, and fertility, with accompanying prayers and calls for assistance by your spirit allies and gods. Such prayers only exist in Christian forms now but creating your own on the spot is perfectly effective so long as you are clear in your intention. Obviously, sensible care should also be taken when using fire in this way to ensure safety—candles lit from a magical fire may be the more practical option in some circumstances.

Another old practice was to leap the fire, an activity popular at Beltane celebrations, where the young men especially would use this as an opportunity to show off their vigour and agility, but again with sensible precautions, its possible for almost anyone to jump or step over a fire for cleansing and blessing, and to receive the vitality the spirit of the fire provides. One way for older or more delicate people to jump the fire is to use the embers, and when a fire is well established to bank it down slightly and drag out a thin line of embers with small low flames to one side, enabling those less able to step neatly over it.

Fire Magic—Prayers

In cultures around the world, fires have always been used for making prayers. The transformative effects of fire and the sight of smoke and heat haze rising up to the sky evoke images of our intentions and messages floating up into the heavens where they can be heard by our gods and ancestors. The Celtic practices of sacred fires at the fire festivals of Imbolc, Beltane, Lughnasadh, and Samhain show an awareness of fire's magical and healing properties; the practice of burning things as offerings and prayers is also long standing. Various things can be used for making prayers with fire: sacred herbs, gathered consciously by the practitioner themselves as green spirit kin will have the best efficacy. However, prayers can also be written on paper or carved into wood. Straw figures like the corn dollies and the traditional last bale of straw known as the Cailleach figure (gathered and made as the final act of reaping the harvest), can be powerful offerings to accompany requests for healing or prosperity. Other effigies of body parts requiring healing for example, may also be burnt, such as carved or sculpted hearts, eyes, or even limbs and organs.

Care must be taken when lighting a ritual fire to respectfully honour the fire spirits before requests are spoken aloud and offerings and any physical representation of the prayer are given to be burned and transmuted into the spirit world via the flames. Sometimes the prayer and the offering are the same thing, e.g., an item carved of wood that will burn well. At other times such as with prayers written on paper, additional offerings seem most appropriate. Above all, there is no rule book. Respect for the spirits and practical considerations need to be combined for the best results.

Saining

A traditional practice in Scotland, *saining* was said to remove illness and ill wishes from a house or area. The practice involved burning branches of juniper and letting the smoke fill the house from top to bottom, until the whole area was dense with smoke, so much so that no one could stay inside. When the house was fully smoked, only then would the doors and windows be opened to let the smoke out, carrying with it all the negative energy and illness. Saining is exactly like modern-day fumigation to remove insect infestations, only it worked on an energetic, spiritual, and emotional level as well. Though wild juniper is endangered these days, it is widely available to cultivate and grow. Burning dried juniper or juniper berries as incense upon a charcoal disk works just as well and provides the perfect alternative to burning sage or smudging, which is a traditional Native America practice. Bunches of juniper can be bound in the same way as a smudge stick and burnt in exactly the same way without cultural appropriation and in a way that honours our Celtic ancestors and with a plant that grows better in cooler northern climates than white sage.

Celtic Sweat Houses

While the Native American sweat lodge is well known, its Northern European equivalents are often overlooked. Known in Ireland until relatively recently (the nineteenth century) as the *teach allais* or *sweat house*, evidence for this practice has been found as far as the Outer Hebrides and as far back in time as the Neolithic era, some 5,000 years ago. In recent centuries, these were mostly beehive-shaped structures made out of stone with a small entrance. Strange structures dating from the bronze age known as *Fulachta fiadh* or *burnt mounds*, which show evidence of the use of fire and water are thought to be ritual sites for sweat houses. Unlike the Native American sweat lodges, these structures were also made of stone and often turfed over for added insulation. A *teach allais* or *Fulachta fiadh* was usually placed near a naturally occurring spring or holy well as a water source. Prior to its use, a fire would be burnt inside it to heat the structure, and then the fire was dragged out and the person seeking healing went in and remained there in the darkness until sufficient sweating had occurred. They would then crawl out and immerse or cover themselves in the cold water from the sacred spring. A wonderful source from the nineteenth century describes it thus:

> Small buildings called sweat-houses are erected, somewhat in the shape of a beehive, constructed with stones and turf, neatly put together; the roof being formed of the same material, with a small hole in the centre. There is also an aperture below, just large enough to admit one person, on hands and knees. When required for use, a large fire is lighted in the middle of the floor, and allowed to burn out, by which time the house has become thoroughly heated; the ashes are then swept away, and the patient goes in, having first taken off his clothes, with the exception of his undergarment, which he hands to a friend outside. The hole in the roof is then covered with a flat stone and the entrance is also closed up with sods, to prevent the admission of air. The patient remains within until he begins to perspire copiously, when (if young and strong) he plunges into the sea, but the aged or weak retire to bed for a few hours.[49]

---

49. *A History of the Island of Rathlin* by Mrs. Grange, Rathlin 1851, Coleraine. http: //irisharchaeology.ie/2012/03/the-sweat-house-at-creevaghbaun-co-galway/.

Constructing a traditional Irish sweat house today is beyond the scope of this book, but it is worth noting that constructing various shelters and willow wood "benders" for temporary use in this way is perfectly reasonable. As the fire is put out after the structure has become sufficiently heated, there is less of the danger than with the Native American sweat lodge—there are no hot rocks to be careful of. While we know of no prayers and rituals being used in these structures in the pre-Christian era, it is extremely unlikely that they were used only for cleansing and the healing of rheumatism. Evidence in Ireland suggests these structures were mostly used in the autumn months, perhaps when a trained healer or druid came through the area, or as some have suggested, they were to be used alongside various hallucinogenic mushrooms that also favour growing in such sites in the autumn months such as fly agaric (*Amanita muscaria*) and so-called magic mushrooms such as the liberty cap, *Psilocybe semilanceata*. It's safe to presume our ancestors in Ireland and the British isles knew of these mushrooms and their effects, but sadly much of that wisdom has now been lost. Modern studies have suggested liberty caps can help in healing depression, PTSD, and even migraines.[50] It's likely they would have been of tremendous psychological and spiritual benefit in the hands of trained and experienced practitioners. Working with such potent plant spirits in the confines of an Irish sweathouse would have been a powerful experience indeed!

Fire Banishing

Fires can be used to consume and transform all sorts of negative energy and are useful in spell work to burn away any cords, candles, poppets, or any physical spell objects once they have performed their purpose. Fire can also be used in ritual to burn off illness or any other negative spirit intrusion.

---

50. Robin Carhart-Harris, Leor Roseman, Mark Bolstridge, et al. "Psilocybin for treatment-resistant depression: fMRI-measured brain mechanisms," *Scienfitic Reports* 7. https://www.nature.com/articles/s41598-017-13282-7.

Fire Blessings

Traditional fire blessings usually involve either leaping the Beltane fire or carrying a fiery brand clockwise around the boundaries of a piece of land. This practice can still be performed today in a more practical manner, by lighting a candle in a suitable holder and asking Brighid to bless the flame. Use your own words for this or try these:

> Great goddess Brighid, bless this flame, bless this candle, may
> your eternal flame burn brightly here and bless this home (or
> space, land, et cetera.)

Take the candle, and lead it clockwise around the house, or space, and clockwise around every room in the house or any other area, making sure the light shines in every dark corner, nook and cranny, or anywhere that needs special attention, such as where people sleep, or where there are old objects that may contain energetic residues. As you go, imagine the flame is a great ray of light that reaches every aspect of the space, clears away any negativity, and fills the space with spiritual as well as literal light.

When you have finished, take the candle to an altar or other central spot and leave it to burn down. Offer your thanks to Brighid for her blessing.

Suitable Woods for Fuel

As well as choosing well-seasoned dry wood, the type of wood that you burn will have an effect upon the success of your fire and the way it burns. In addition, certain woods are traditionally taboo to burn, or can have added magical or spiritual significance—good for ritual fires with a specific purpose.

The following is a traditional English folk song that lists the most common woods and their burning properties:

Traditional Tales
The Woodcutter's Song

Oak logs will warm you well
That are old and dry

Logs of pine will sweetly smell
But the sparks will fly
Birch logs will burn too fast
And chestnut scarce at all, sir
Hawthorne logs are good to last
That are cut well in the fall, sir
Holly logs will burn like wax
You could burn them green
Elm logs burn like smouldering flax
With no flame to be seen
Beech logs for winter time
Yew logs as well, sir
Green elder logs it is a crime
For any man to sell, sir
Pear logs and apple logs
They will scent your room
And cherry logs across the dogs
Smell like flowers a bloom
But ash logs smooth and gray
Buy them green or old, sir
And buy up all that come your way
For they're worth their weight in gold sir'[51]

Taboos

There are numerous taboos in Celtic tree lore, often for very practical reasons. It is never a good idea to burn yew—while the toxicity in the wood is commonly thought to not present a problem when burned, especially in log burners where the smoke is taken well away from anyone sitting by it, I have known several occasions where people have become sick and experi-

---

51. The Woodcutter's Song—also known as "Logs to Burn" and "The Dartmoor Log Song." There are many versions of this British folk song; this version was published first in volume 159 of the British magazine *Punch* in 1920, and is listed as being by Honor Goodheart but is of disputed authorship and may have been adapted from other sources. https://archive.org /details/punchvol158a159lemouoft/page/898.

enced severe psychological distress and terrifying nightmares when breathing in yew smoke. Yew is highly toxic and care should be taken when handling it. Woodcarvers and archers using yew bows seem to have no trouble, but there is plenty of anecdotal evidence of it effecting those cutting the wood when it's fresh, and the leaves and berries are highly toxic. Care needs to be taken when handling yew, especially when children are around. Equally, yew is a highly magical tree and a powerful spirit in its own right, intimately connected to the dead and the otherworld. For these reasons, the tree and its wood need to be treated with care and respect. While it burns hot and smells pleasant, it can unintentionally evoke powerful underworld forces with ensuing, undesirable results. Be warned!

Another taboo is burning elder—in fact, it is taboo to ever cut the elder without first seeking permission and offering recompense to its spirit, the Elder Mother. Elders are closely connected to faeries and powerful natural magic (this is not a tree for Tinkerbelle!)—"the good folk" who must be treated with respect and care at all times, and can be terrible if crossed. A tradition from folklore suggests that you should seek the Elder Mother's permission by saying:

> Elder tree, Elder Mother, please may I have some of your wood,
> and you may have some of mine when it grows in the forest.

This petition is done essentially to trick the spirit; I would say it is far better to make the tree a simple offering of some water or a small bowl of honey, speaking to it and letting it know your intention at least a day before cutting it—never burn it. However, the pith inside the elder is very soft, and a thin, straight, hollowed out elder branch can make a good blowpipe to blow a fire back to life.

Magical Woods for Fuel

There is a host of lore in the Celtic tradition about trees and their magical properties; for an extensive exploration of the subject, please see my book *Celtic Tree Magic* (Llewellyn 2014). To cover the subject briefly I believe it's important to remember that every tree, plant, or other living thing we work with has its inherent spirit, and to work well with any living thing magically depends on our relationship with these spirits. Therefore, it is always a good idea to know what wood you are burning for a ritual fire and where it came from. Best practice is to cut it with an offering and thanks for its gift and thank it again when you burn it. Where this isn't possible, take time to connect with the spirits who once dwelled in your cut logs or fallen branches by spending a few breaths to become present to them. Thank them as your green kin for their gift as fuel, at least.

Knowing which type of tree you are burning can also have an effect upon your ritual or magic, and seeking the best trees for your purpose is a good idea, again making sure you are as conscious of what you are doing as possible. The following is a simple reference to the main magical trees in the Celtic tradition in addition to their uses in a ritual fire.

Oak: The tree of sovereignty and the green man. Oak's name in Gaelic, Dara, is where we get the name druid, from deru wid, someone who has the wisdom of the oak. Best for all sacred fires, especially at Beltane and Samhain, but should be honoured as a treasured resource—oak is a slow-growing tree, so efforts should be made for its sustainable and responsible use.

Hawthorn: The queen of the May, associated with faeries and female magic as well as the heart and feelings. Good for love spells, faerie connection, healing, and to raise life force.

Birch: This tree burns quickly and is the first of the Irish ogham alphabet. Associated with fresh starts, cleansing, and rectification. Burn to initiate a new cycle in life, at baby blessings, and in new homes.

Pine: Use pine to cleanse illness and clear stuck energy. Pine is associated with the upper world and calling in air spirits, such as eagle and buzzard.

Apple: This tree is associated with the Celtic otherworld, Avalon, where souls seek healing and regeneration. Burn for healing magic and for rituals of reconciliation and compassion as well as sexual magic, and marriages.

Ash: Ash is a powerful magical ally generally and in many ways the best wood as fuel; however, ash is on its way to becoming an endangered tree due to the disease called Ash Dieback in the UK and Europe; it also has problems with infestations of the Emerald Ash Borer in the US. This wood should be used responsibly and sustainably—check all restrictions regarding this tree in your area and take steps to honour this tree whenever it is used.

Six

OUR GREEN KIN

We are surrounded by plants, fungi, lichens, and trees in all but the most inhospitable parts of the world. Wherever we are, there will be some kind of plant making its way into the light, whether it be a vast swathe of forest, or a dandelion breaking through a crack in the pavement. Indigenous traditions all around the world make use of plants and trees for both healing and magical and spiritual purposes. In the Celtic lands of the north are a great many plant resources to call upon. These magical herbs or "power plants" can address almost any need, and working with them can bind us more closely into relationship with our environment, the spirits of place and our ancestors than we ever imagined, as well as being of use to our practice and of service to our communities.

Magical Plants and Trees as Allies and Helpers

Wise women and healers in the British Isles have used herbs for healing and magic for thousands of years; nature provides us with all the support and allies we could ever need if we align ourselves with her rhythms and values and approach the green world as friends and kin rather than as passive consumers. If we are able to grow and tend to our friends in the plant world and provide them a home in our gardens and windowsills, so much the better. As well, foraging and knowing our landscapes will meet all our needs—magically, it is possible to work with a plant and not even use any of its physical matter, leaving no trace on our environment at all.

When we take the time to connect to the green world around us, we inevitably engage in a process which slows us down and shows us the world in a new way that goes beyond our everyday perspective. The small details, the myriad of plants around us, and the minutiae of their everyday lives has much to teach us about the ground beneath our feet. Take the time to notice what grows around you wild and untended. Is your environment a timeless Eden or an urban battle for survival? In some areas, only the toughest weeds get a look in, sometimes doused with chemicals from city landscapers in attempts to eradicate even their small lives from encroaching on to the pavement and concrete sprawl. Grasses, dandelions, and the odd daisy are the heroes of the green world, surviving almost everywhere. Buddleia, oxeye daisies, and buttercups are also urban toughies; together with nettles and dock, these may make considerable headway on roadside verges and motorway embankments. However, when we take a moment to consider them, we can discover a whole host of power plants; spirits honouring the earth wherever they are, holding on, giving food to insects and supporting tiny eco-systems, and providing healing spirit medicine to the powers of place.

For example, dandelion is a nutrient-rich wild food, excellent for helping to clear toxins from the body, and will magically help us to learn resilience and to see the joy in tough circumstances.

If we get to know our environment intimately, get to know all the plants and trees that grow near us, naturally, as well as the ones that thrive in our cultivated gardens and parks, then we can get insight into the powers of place themselves, we can discover how our landscape expresses itself, what its needs and priorities are. Sometimes in the city these will reveal its attempts to keep the life force of an area and its inhabitants thriving, but in other greener spaces it can show us an area's unique flavour and personality—what it chooses to express and manifest.

Here in the British Somerset levels, we are surrounded by willow and alder trees—they will grow wild everywhere with ease. The willow is a great watery lunar spirit; healing and easing pain, it teaches flexibility and the importance of our dreams—a suitable ally to greet weary pilgrims to the ancient isle of Glastonbury and the otherworldly destination of Avalon with which it is so closely associated. By contrast, alder is strong and teaches about service and sacrificing oneself for others—it was the wood of choice for the shields for Celtic warriors, its wood turning red when exposed to air to bleed in their stead. Alder wood will keep intact even growing at the edges of the water. With its feet in the marsh, it will endure and survive and hold strong, preserving itself and what it holds dear, keeping grounded even in the midst of emotional, watery overwhelm or rapid spiritual expansion. By contacting the spirits of the plants around us, and learning about their properties whether medicinally, botanically, folklorically, even mythologically we can develop our own understanding of them, and the workings of the genius loci that they embody.

Buddleia, otherwise known as the butterfly bush, provides great magical and spiritual assistance when trying to help those with depression, and its great warrior spirit bravely tackles negative energies and sends healing out across a whole landscape, drawing more life force to an area. Known in Britain as the bombsite bush, it was one of the first plants to grow on areas hit by bombs in the second World War—it will bring life and healing back anywhere that has known trauma, desolation or destruction. It is so successful that some types of Buddleia are now thought of as invasive. Buddleia attracts masses of butterflies and is a vital food source for them, so they have an essential place in any wildlife garden. Additionally, they also attract those transformational energies represented by the butterfly into an area. It therefore has a place in any spell or healing work that needs to break up and transform negative patterns or stuck energy and bring about positive change. Anyone who has ever seen a buddleia in flower on a desolate building site can see it working this magic by itself.

Ways to Connect with Plant Spirits

Visit wild green spaces. Plant a garden. Join a community gardening or tree planting project. Visit the forest. Grow your own food- even salad and herbs on your windowsill. Study the healing herbs and their applications. Meditate with trees. Encourage wildlife by planting pollinators. Eat a vegetarian diet, whenever possible. So long as it is safe, try an herbal diet or fast from time to time to connect with specific powerful plant spirits, by ingesting only a particular plant for a day or two. Journey to meet plant spirits in your inner vision. Breathe with the trees. Glean seeds, berries, and nuts, and sow them in pots to redistribute.

☽ EXERCISE ☾
JOURNEY TO MEET A PLANT SPIRIT

If you can, perform this exercise in front of the plant or tree itself; if you can't do this, you can fix an image of the plant in your inner eye, and with your intention journey to meet it.

Sitting comfortably, close your eyes and take three deep breaths. Feel the ground beneath you, your energy and intention sinking deeper and connecting you to the land below, the land within. Imagine that you have a path of pale stone leading ahead of you, which leads directly to the spirit aspect of the plant in front of you. The path may be short and direct, but if it wanders take note of all you see as every aspect of the journey is a communication from the plant itself.

Send a message of friendship to the plant and be patient: every plant spirit is different and will have their own boundaries and ways of communicating. See if you can accept and experience the plant just as it is without any preconceived ideas or projections.

After a time, it may be appropriate to breathe with the plant—focus on sending your breath to it, and accept its breath in return as an exchange of energy and information to connect you on a deeper nonverbal level. Communion and communication are key.

If you wish, you may ask the plant spirit any questions you may have, but again strive to be open minded in your understanding of the answers you may receive.

After a time, thank the plant spirit and return along the path. Feel the air in your lungs and send your intention and will to returning you to your body. Open your eyes and wiggle your fingers and toes, feeling yourself fully returned and present.

You may like to record your experiences in a journal.

❱ PRACTICAL ❰
SENSING WITH YOUR HANDS

Another interesting way to work with plants and to get to know their spirit forms is to learn to feel their energy with your hands. There have been numerous practices among the Celts of using the fingertips or the palms to feel energetic qualities and conditions, most notably for healing or divination. The ancient Irish practice of *Dichotal do Chonnaib* may have involved this sort of practice sometimes with a wand or a staff as a mobile plant ally carried with you, in addition to your hands' sensitivity to help your body tune in to the finer subtle energies.

With your palm facing the plant, slowly extend your arm and hand towards it. Be still and quiet, allowing a space and calm receptivity to come over you. See if you can feel it shift when you sense something beyond your own body. Often this is a tingling or feeling of heat or pressure in your palm or fingertips. When you feel it, move your hand around the plant, keeping the same distance. Then move gently forwards and back, seeing if you can feel the edge of its aura and what the difference is within and outside it. Take your time with this; it needs plenty of patient sensitivity and may need some practice. In time, you will be able to easily feel when you are in a tree or plants aura or energy field, and this can be developed further still until you can sense the mood or temperament of the plant, and even receive clearer impressions using your inner eye. If you work with a wand or staff for this work, take note as well of what your ally may be telling you, and look out for a difference in sensation between the hand holding the staff and the one that is not.

Wands and Staffs

Many people like to work with a traditional wand, or have a tall staff with them during a ceremony, but what is often overlooked is that these sorts of tools are, in the best cases, living tree spirit allies who work with us and help direct our intentions, or more accurately, create connections with other spirit intelligences to attract and draw to us what we are seeking to manifest.

Making a wand can be very simple, and while some choose to carve and decorate their wands and staffs, this isn't necessary, although it can make them very attractive and add extra energy thanks to the power in the act of decorating, as well as the power of any symbols or additions such as crystals. That said, the primary use of a wand is as a mobile and physically present plant ally, where the spirit of the tree has agreed to continue to work with you through the wood.

Most wands or staffs are cut from a chosen tree, but this doesn't have to be the case. Fallen wood, when gathered and chosen in communion with the indwelling plant spirit can be even more powerful than cutting living wood and of course does no harm to the tree itself as a bonus. In many cases choosing wood for a wand in this manner may be preferable, but keep in mind that every tree and every tree spirit will be slightly different. The important issue is to be aware and present, working closely and respectfully with the tree spirit, building our relationship with it as an ally, and following its guidance as much as we are able.

☽ PRACTICAL ☾
JOURNEY TO SEEK A WAND
OR A STAFF ALLY

This exercise is best done in the woods or forest where you plan to find your chosen piece. Its best if you know the area well, but any woodland that you feel attracted to and have any relevant permissions to collect wood from is fine.

Find a place where you can sit, undisturbed for twenty to thirty minutes. Once you are seated comfortably, take three deep slow breaths. Imagine that you are slowly growing roots into the earth beneath you. Either aloud or in your inner vision, announce to the trees around you that you come in friendship and respect and seek their counsel. Slowly feel yourself pull in some of the life force of the land beneath you. Drink it in through your roots and feel it raise up your spine. Drink in the air around you as well, and the sunlight filtering through the tree canopy above, let yourself slow and be still, breathing with the trees.

When you are ready, see ahead of you a pale stone path. Ask that you be met by a tree ally, a friend and guide to your work with the trees, and set off along the path, through the forest as it is in your inner eye. Soon you will be met by your guide, who may take any form but will usually appear near a tree or resemble one themselves. Spend some time getting to know your guide. Ask how you can learn more about working with trees and plants, and ask them to work with you often so that you can deepen your practice. When you are ready, also ask them to guide you to a tree in the physical forest that you can work with and make a wand or staff.

If they agree, open your eyes. After making sure you still feel grounded, walk through the physical trees now and ask your guide to accompany you. Try to be aware of any sensations you may have or guidance you may receive. Be gentle with yourself as this can take time and practice.

Eventually you may be led to a specific tree that feels right to you and may have a special feel about it. What sort of tree is it? Before proceeding, you must know this and may need to look it up. Spend some time with your guide and this tree, again taking plenty of time. Return to your inner vision, breathing slowly with the tree and your guide. Is this tree your guide's physical representative? Is your guide the spirit of this tree, or something else? You may need to sit patiently and ask to meet the spirit of this particular tree next.

When you feel you are in contact with the spirit of this tree, again ask to befriend it, ask that you may work together and if it is prepared to share some of its wood. Be sensitive here, be open to its communication, you may need to return and try again another day. Trees take time. Eventually you may be guided to cut a piece or find just what you need at its feet. Ask that the spirit of the tree inhabits the wood you use, to work with you through this piece. The tree spirit will still dwell in the tree but will also be with you when called. Feel in your chest and belly, and check in your inner vision, is the tree willing to do this? Is there an indwelling spirit in the piece you have chosen?

Always thank the tree and your tree guide, and give the tree an offering of your love and care. Spend time with the tree long after you have taken the wood you need, honour it as a friend.

When it is time to disconnect from your tree spirit work, just thank your guide and the tree, and see yourself in your inner eye walking back along the path, back into your body. Any part of you that had wandered into spirit to do this work will return with your intent. Stamp your feet and eat and drink to fully ground yourself.

Traditional Tales

Celtic lore and legend hold many clues about how plants and trees were worked with for both magic and healing in ancient times, showing frequently that these two disciplines were close if not overlapping. Herbal remedies were usually accompanied with healing charms and prayers, and more than a little magic was used in most cases together with practical skills. The following two traditional tales are probably the best examples of the Celtic healing tradition and its roots in a distant, now semi-mythological past.

The Story of Airmid's Cloak (Irish)

Dian Cecht, the Irish god of healing, had won great renown by his works. At the battle of Magh Tuiredh Nuada, the king had lost his arm, and thus his kingship as the king had to be perfect in all ways. However, Dian Cecht made him an arm of silver, and after that he was known as Nuada Airgetlám, *the silver handed*. But Dian Cecht's reputation as the greatest healer of them all was challenged by his son, Miach, who by his art grew a new arm of flesh and blood and bone for Nuada, restoring him to wholeness. Dian Cecht became jealous and tried to slay his son four times, but each time Miach healed himself, until the fourth and final time, when Cian Cecht struck him with a sword into his brain. Dian Cecht lamented his deeds and buried his son, and from his grave 365 herbs grew, each a cure for a different ailment. Miach's sister, Airmed gathered the herbs on her cloak, so that their uses could be known, but Dian Cecht grew jealous again and scattered them to the winds, so that none but those who already knew their secret could use them.

In the second battle of Mag Tuiredh, Dian Cecht had made a great cauldron of healing, now a well called Slane near Moytura, where the warriors of the Tuatha De Danann could be healed of their wounds. Some sources say he scattered the herbs into these waters to make a magical healing brew. However, it is to Airmed most healers pray, that she may gift them the knowledge to help and to restore those afflicted by illness or wounding with the knowledge of the herbs she gathered.

☽ PRACTICAL ☾
CALLING UPON AIRMED

The goddess Airmed can be called upon at any time to assist you in understanding and improving your healing skills, especially with regards to all herbal medicine and growing healing herbs, as well as finding the right herbal remedy for your needs.

If you wish to develop your herbal skills, take a large green candle and inscribe her name upon it, leaving it out among your plants overnight to absorb their energy. Then when preparing your herbs or potions light the candle and call upon Airmed to assist you. You might like to try these words or use your own.

> Goddess Airmed, mistress of healing and herbal wisdom,
> help me to remember the ancient ways of the plant spirits

and their virtues, that I too may learn to bring wholeness and healing! Beannachtai, blessed be![52]

Take three deep breaths and call her to you with your heart and clear intention. Then as you gather your herbs, hang them to dry, or prepare them in any other way, continue to speak to her and ask that she bless your work and the powers of the herbs themselves. If you are preparing an herbal tisane or salve for example, make a prayer to Airmed as you do so, and then take a moment placing your hands over the brew or mixture, and ask her to bless and empower your medicine for the best healing ends. Try drawing energy up from the earth into your hands and projecting it into the herbs to add extra energy.

The Physicians of the Myddfai (Welsh)

The three pillars of knowledge, with which the Gwyddonaid (men of knowledge—druids) were acquainted, and which they bore in memory from the beginning: the first a knowledge of Divine things…the second, a knowledge of the course of the stars, their names and kinds, and the order of times: the third, a knowledge of the names and use of the herbs of the field, and of their application in practice, in medicine and in religious worship. These were preserved in the memorials of vocal song, and in the memorials of times, before there were bards of degree and chair.[53]

The physicians of the Myddfai were amongst the most famous herbal healers in all of medieval Britain. Based in the village of Myddfai in Carmarthenshire, the earliest records of them come from 1234 when Riwallon and his sons attended to Rhys Gryg, Prince of Deheubarth, when he was wounded in battle. This line of herbal healers continued until 1739, and details of their work including instruction on their herbal preparations were recorded in the *Red Book of Hergest* (1382), making it a valuable resource for us today.

---

52. *Beannachtai:* literally *blessings* in Irish. We use the Irish here to honour the Irish origin of Airmed.

53. John Pugh, translator. *The Physicians of the Myddfai*, 1861. Reprinted by Llanerch. 1993, ix.

According to legend, the physicians healing knowledge came from an ancient otherworldly source, as did their bloodline. Llyn y Fan Fach is a lake near the village, and one day a young man was passing the lake when he saw a beautiful young woman emerge from the waters leading a small herd of beautiful cattle. He at once fell in love and begged her to marry him, for she was clearly one of the Tylwyth Teg, the faerie folk. She agreed on one condition: if he should strike her three times, she would leave him forever. The young man swore he would never strike her, and they lived happily for many years, raising three sons in a house near the village. But the husband could not keep his word. He struck her three times: once for laughing at a funeral, another for crying at a wedding, and the third time when he tapped her on the shoulder to get her attention. She left for the lake once more, taking her cattle with her. She returned only to teach her sons her healing magic, which they passed on from generation to generation for hundreds of years, becoming the greatest healers in the land.[54]

Connecting With Our Ancestral Healers and the Healing Spirits of the Land

Read the old stories as much as you can, and learn as much of the old lore on herbs and healing as possible, but remember these are living traditions and the spirits who taught us in the earliest days remain, and can be sought out by us once more.

To do this work, you need to have a close relationship with your local landscape and be used to working with spirit allies.

Go out and identify a special place in nature for you to meditate—a healing well or a sacred place with a tradition of healing is excellent. If this isn't practical then you will need to make a pilgrimage to such a place at some point and connect to the place in your inner vision after this.

If you are able, visit the place regularly and leave offerings of song and poetry or some biodegradable gift to the spirits there. Homemade baked goods are traditional gifts, as are cream and honey. Settle yourself in a

---

54. There are several versions of this tale. This one is collated from several sources and retold by the author.

place where you can sit comfortably and uninterrupted for up to an hour. Breathe slow and deeply to calm and centre yourself. Close your eyes or let your focus soften.

When you are ready, call aloud to the spirits of place and ask for a guide to come to you to help develop your healing skills. Remember this guide may take many forms, and the first things they may draw attention to may be how to attend to your own healing of mind, body, or soul. Be open to their promptings, and remember you are always free to accept or deny their advice. Know also that if you ignore their help or question it, you may lose their support in the future.

Let your senses sink into the land beneath you. In your inner vision, see yourself gently going within both yourself and into the spirit landscape of where you are seated.

How does the place where you sit look and feel with this inner vision? Allow plenty of space for your guide to come to you—they may come quickly, and have clear guidance for you or you may be told you need to come and ask another time, or that other things are required before you undertake this work. Remember this is receiving guidance from spirit and you need to respect and befriend them—demanding knowledge or anything else from spirits is never advisable. Effective work stems from building a mutually positive relationship over time, but having a spirit teacher (whether of the land or those who walked it before you) is a treasure beyond measure.

A Celtic Wild Herbal

There are a great many healing plants in the Celtic tradition, and others that can be found all over the world. Each of these has a unique spirit that should be befriended for the best results, and not all healing herbs can be listed here, but what follows is a selection of some of the most powerful and useful green allies and can form a basis for further work.

Mistletoe—Viscum album
Drua–Lus (Irish/ Scots Gaelic) "the druid's herb"; Uchelwydd (Welsh)

Mistletoe is perhaps the most famous plant associated with Druidry. A parasitic evergreen plant, Mistletoe likes to grow mostly on apple, hawthorn, and ash trees, but is most prized when it grows upon the oak. Its milky white berries are full of white sticky liquid much like semen and as such it may well be and have been considered the semen of the sky or oak god, most probably Taranis.

Mistletoe can be found across Europe, North Africa, and parts of Asia. It grows in a recognisable spherical shape in the branches of trees. Its leaves are thick and leathery, oval in shape, and its tiny yellow-green flowers appear from February to April.

Pliny the elder tells us that the Iron Age druids used to gather the mistletoe from an oak on the sixth day of the new moon, probably the new moon nearest the winter solstice. They would cut the bough using a golden sickle (probably more likely bronze but still with solar connotations) and gather it in a hide or cloak before it touched the ground, else its' magic would be lost.

Lindow Man, the Iron Age body discovered in a bog in northwest England in 1984, showed traces of mistletoe in his stomach. His well-groomed appearance led archaeologists to believe he was a man of high status, possibly an honoured sacrifice ritually fed mistletoe before his death.

Mistletoe is usually associated with fertility, from its Iron Age ceremonies to the popularity of the Christmas tradition of kissing beneath it. It has been used in some parts of England as a charm to increase fertility by hanging it over the bed or tying it to a woman's wrist or waist. Mistletoe has been found to have immune system enhancing properties and has been used to fight or prevent cancer. In Europe and Britain, it is used as herbal medicine to treat arthritis and high blood pressure, however it is a powerful plant that is poisonous if taken in excess or if one has certain pre-existing conditions or are taking certain medications. It is best avoided without the guidance of a fully trained medical herbalist, and should never be given to children or pets. European mistletoe tea and herbal remedies are available for sale in the UK and

Europe, however American mistletoe, *Phoradendron serotinum,* is a very different plant and ingestion is best avoided entirely without more scientific study.

Juniper—*Juniperus communis*
Aitil (Irish), Aiteann (Scots Gaelic), Merywen (Welsh)

Juniper can be found across the Northern Hemisphere, with a preference for chalk or limestone heathland. Although it is endangered in Britain, it still grows wild prolifically in Ireland. It grows in a distinctive, craggy twisted shape up to 5 meters tall, with deep green-blue needles and red berries.

After the last Ice Age, Juniper was probably the first tree to recolonise the land, and its needles and wood contain powerful antiseptic ingredients and carry a rich woody green scent prized in aromatherapy.

Juniper's cleansing properties are considered magical as well as physical, and it is also a highly protective herb. Pouches of juniper were hung from the rafters of houses and barns for protection, and in Scotland juniper was burnt in a tradition called *saining* to ritually cleanse a home at New Year as well as in the run up to Beltane. This practice was also popular in some parts of Cornwall and Brittany. Sprigs of juniper were carried or nailed to doors as protection against theft and to rid a house of ghosts.

Juniper is used to make delicious gin as well as a strengthening and cleansing tea. It is also used in baths to stimulate the circulation and cleanse the blood. Juniper boughs were sometimes used to fill the cavity walls in houses, as extra insulation as well as protection and to deter insects, and juniper pills were taken well into the twentieth century to induce abortions.

Vervain—*Verbena officinalis*
Trombhad (Scots Gaelic), Yn Lus–"the herb," Yn Ard Lus–"the chief herb" (Manx)

Vervain is a short woody perennial whose tiny lilac flowers appear in May. It has long, thin, spiky toothed leaves, and rarely grows above about 80cm (2ft). The leaves are bitter and astringent, and the flowers have no perfume.

This plant is easy to overlook, but is one of the most powerful and sacred plants in the Celtic tradition, going by many names: the Enchanters Plant, the Herb of Grace, Holy Wort, and the Wizard's plant. According to Pliny the elder, Vervain is one of the four plants most sacred to the druids, the others being mistletoe, silago (possibly fir club moss), and samulus which could be several plants, but most likely water pimpernel or pasque flower. The druids gathered vervain just before it flowered, at the dark of the moon. Holding the plant up to the constellation Sirius, which may have had associations to do with the underworld and the faery hounds, the Cwn Annwn, Vervain was cut with a sickle and held up with the left hand, and an offering of honey would then be given to the earth in its place in thanks.

Vervain was considered a cure-all to Iron Age druids and was used in Gaul for divination and prophecy. It was also widely used for purification of sacred spaces, including some say the temple of Solomon. Roman soldiers also carried vervain for protection. Today is it often used by druids and Celtic practitioners in lustral baths and to ritually cleanse magical tools. Commonly used to increase *Awen*, or divine inspiration. It can be steeped in oil for anointing tools and the third eye, or drunk prior to scrying or other visionary work. Bunches of vervain can also be used to ritually sweep a space or decorate the altar.

Mugwort—Artemisia vulgaris
Mongach meisce (Irish), Liath–lus (Scots and Irish Gaelic)–"the grey herb"

Mugwort is the common name for various forms of the Artemisia family, although *Artemisia vulgaris* is the British and Irish form. Artemisia grows across Europe, North America, as well as in some parts of Africa and Asia. Growing up to four feet tall, it is a successful weed as well as an attractive garden plant that self-seeds easily. Its spiky, many-lobed leaves are dark green on top and downy white or grey underneath, although variegated strains can also be found.

Mugwort is most often associated with dreams and in particular, lucid dreaming, where the dreamer may encounter the gods and spirits and learn from them. Mugwort placed under the pillow or drank as an infusion can induce very vivid dreams which will often alert of deeper issues in need of healing, or warn of danger and deception. Sacred to the moon and huntress goddess Artemis as well as the goddess Hecate, mugwort is the friend of all women and helpful for women's issues magically and medicinally. A powerful emmenagogue, mugwort stimulates menstruation and has been used in larger quantities as an abortifacient. It should therefore be avoided during pregnancy, but it also has uses in labour in the hands of one suitably trained.

Mugwort traditionally also is said to be able to relieve fatigue and even give the wearer endless energy. Pliny tells us "The wayfaring man that has the herb tied about him feels no weariness at all, and he can never be hurt by any poisonous medicine, by any wild beast neither by the sun itself."

Mugwort leaves have been used in Chinese medicine for centuries, bound into bundles or moxas which are burnt at one end and used as a heat application for rheumatism or along meridians or acupuncture points.

Mugwort has often been used bound in bunches as smudge sticks, alone or with other herbs as it is considered cleansing and protective. Hang bunches of mugwort over doors for protection and sachets or pouches of mugwort are good for ensuring safety when travelling. Cooled infusions of mugwort, especially if they are made with fresh spring water, are excellent for ritually cleansing and cleaning magical tools.

St John's Wort—Hypericum perforatum
Lus na Maighdine Muire, Lus Colaim Chille (Irish)

St John's wort can be found across the UK, Ireland, Europe, and the northern United States; it is sometimes considered invasive. A perennial herb found in open woods, rough grass, and even roadside verges, it can grow up to two feet tall, with small oval leaves and bright yellow starshaped flowers. The new stems can be red only turning green later with age. The plant is clump forming and prefers full sun but can grow perfectly well in partial shade, and it reproduces abundantly from seed as well as from runners.

St John's wort is an important plant in the Celtic tradition, associated with St John's day, or Midsummer, June 24. Tradition says it was burned inside the midsummer or summer solstice fires lit to bless and purify the community and their fields. It is a highly magical plant carried to ensure good luck and protection, as well as to ease a worried mind or help various forms of mental illness although care should always be taken in severe cases. Closely connected to the sun, St John's wort can be made into useful herbal medicines for depression as well as the healing of nerve damage in conditions like sciatica, aching muscles, burns, as well as cuts and grazes. It heals and rejuvenates the skin and reduces scars, although advice should be sought when taking prescription medicines, and the user should avoid exposure to strong sunlight when using it for the skin. Aside from physical ailments, it is as a defence against unwelcome spirits that St John's wort is most famous. As late as 1919, it was used in Ireland to ease the torment of "fantastical spirits" and was sprinkled around the home to protect from malicious faeries. It was also called St Columba's herb, and according to the saint's biographer, Adamnan, the saint used to carry a packet of it under his arm to assist in his "tussles with demons."

Comfrey—*Symphytum officinalis*
Compar (Irish), Meacan Dubh (Scots Gaelic)
"the dark plant," Lus na cnamh briste (Irish)

This is an upright, bushy perennial with bristly, spear-shaped reticulated leaves, and pale cream or purple bell-like flowers. Native to the UK and Ireland, it is common throughout northern Europe and North America. Comfrey likes to grow near rivers and streams or any damp ground, but its happy enough in most environments where it can get some water and can spread widely.

Comfrey is one of the most useful healing herbs. It contains a chemical called allantoin which promotes healing in connective tissues, and it has long held a reputation for being the best herb for sprains, bruises, abrasions and broken bones. One of its old names is bone-set or knit-bone due to its almost miraculous properties in this area. A few years ago, research suggested it was dangerous to take comfrey internally in teas and tinctures due to possible liver damage, but this was commonly misunderstood as someone would have to take extremely large quantities of the herb for it to be harmful. Comfrey was eaten liberally as a healthy green during the second world war without ill effects. None the less, in the hands of less experienced practitioners, internal use should be limited to the odd cup of comfrey tea to ease aches and pains, and only when no existing liver condition is present. That said, it can be applied externally quite liberally without concern, so long as there is no infection of wounds, etc. Comfrey's healing abilities are so strong that wounds can close over infections or alien matter still present in open cuts unless the area has been cleaned carefully and effectively beforehand. Comfrey has a long and ancient use in folkloric medicine, even being used to line shoes in medieval times to ease aching feet.

Comfrey is an excellent green ally in the garden, as it works to attract bees and butterflies, and can be used to make a top-quality green manure or organic fertilizer by soaking the leaves in a bucket of water until it goes brown.

Comfrey grows very deep roots and is magically very grounding. Try adding it to a bath after magical work to cleanse and earth away any negative energies. Traditionally it is attributed to the planet Saturn and is also considered highly protective. Comfrey root sachets are considered useful for spells of protection whilst travelling and can also be placed in luggage or hung from the mirror in a car for similar purposes. It is also sometimes used to help clear away unhealthy relationships and in tandem with mugwort for use in divination.

Meadowsweet—*Filipendula ulmaria*
Crios Chù Chulainn, criosan Chù Chulainn, "the belt of Chu Chulainn"—(Scots Gaelic) Airgead luachra, "rush silver," (Irish)

Meadowsweet is a perennial herb that grows throughout the UK and Ireland as well as most of Europe; it has also been introduced and naturalised in Northern America. Growing up to 1.25 m it loves damp places, such as the banks of rivers and marshy ground. It has masses of tiny frothy creamy white flowers which grow in clusters and are deliciously scented with a perfume that is somewhere between almond and vanilla. The pinnate and sometimes serrated leaves are upright and dark green on the upper side, and much paler and downy underneath.

While meadowsweet can be found in damp meadows, its name is derived not from meadows but from mead—the plant is used to flavour several varieties of mead especially in Scandinavia. It's a highly useful medicinal plant as well as a highly magical one. Chemically, it contains salicylic acid, flavone glycosides, essential oils, and tannins. Meadowsweet has been used medicinally for centuries and is one source of the modern medicine aspirin. It is useful for easing aches and pains, calming indigestion and upset stomachs, and lowering fevers. It also has culinary uses, as an addition to jams, pies, and preserves. Magically, meadowsweet is used to bless couples and especially wedding ceremonies, but also to represent various goddesses, especially the Welsh Blodeuwedd who was created, or made into human form, by the magician Gwydion using meadowsweet, broom, and oak flowers.

Meadowsweet's Gaelic name, *criosan Chù Chulainn*, *Chu Culainn's belt*, is derived from the story of the hero of Ulster, where the warrior would enter into a battle fury and was unable to calm down until he'd been dunked into a vat of water infused with the herb. Its cooling, feminine energy was the only thing that would break his aggressive power, and he kept some of the flowers in his belt ever after to honour it. According to Elizabethan herbalist John Gerard, "the smell thereof makes the heart merrie and joyful and delighteth the senses." It was also a favourite herb of queen Elizabeth I, and she particularly requested it was strewn about her floors for perfume. Meadowsweet was found in the Bronze Age burial tomb discovered at Forteviot (*Fothair Tabhaicht*) in Perth, Scotland discovered in 2009, providing the first evidence that flower wreaths were laid in prehistoric burials. There is also extensive evidence that the plant has been used in brewing to add flavour since the Neolithic period.

Magically, meadowsweet is used for protection, especially of women, to ease sadness and sorrow, uplift the senses, and bring in love and sensual delight. As such, it is useful in love and healing spells as well as ceremonies and celebrations honouring wild or maiden goddesses. It can also be used to help people break new ground in their lives and overcome constraints and expectations put upon them as they search for their sacred truths.

This is a gentle yet determined herb with an energy that can support those feeling unseen and yet can have a profound effect, especially with women seeking to know themselves better, or for men seeking to make peace with the feminine in their lives. Try herbal sachets of meadowsweet in healing or spell work or taken as a tea or tisane in ceremonies and celebrations. It also helps to ease indigestion, menstrual cramps, aches, pains, and fevers, and support women's nerves and wellbeing during stress or exhaustion. Avoid if sensitive to aspirin.

Woad—*Isatis tinctoria*
Glaisin (Irish), Guirmean, Glas –Ius, Glastam (Scots–Gaelic), Glesyn (Welsh)

Woad is a biennial flowering plant in the family Brassicaceae, which includes cabbage and broccoli. It can grow up to 1m tall, has long oblong leaves up to 10cm in length and flowers in groups of four loose bright yellow petals. Its many names all refer to it being the "blue plant," due to the important blue dye that may be extracted from it. It flowers from June to September, when it sets seed. Woad prefers chalky soils but grows well in many conditions across central and western Europe, central Asia to eastern Siberia, and now across North America where it is sometimes considered invasive.

The blue indigo dye is extracted from the leaves by steeping them in water with soda ash or lime. Caesar describes the Britons as using woad as a body paint in battle, in time leading to the name Picts, or the "painted people" for the northern Britons living in what is now Scotland who were especially known for this practice:

> Most of the inland inhabitants do not grow corn, but live on
> milk and flesh, and are clad with skins. All the Britons indeed
> dye themselves with Woad, which occasions a bluish colour,
> and thereby have a more terrifying appearance in battle.[55]

Woad is an interesting plant: it has the ability to appear one way but produce an almost opposite effect in its alchemical transformation from yellow and green plant to blue dye. Evidence of its use goes back to the Neolithic era, and it seems to have been in wide use in Europe during the Iron Age. Textiles dyed with woad were found in the high-status Celtic Iron Age buri-

---

55. Caesar, Macdevitt, *Gallic Wars* section XIX.

als from the Hallstatt region, such as the Hochdorf Chieftain's Grave and at Hohmichele. Its importance as a dye continued well into the medieval period.

Medicinally, woad is highly astringent and works well as a styptic useful for stopping bleeding, likely a useful side effect of its application as war paint. It is used widely in Traditional Chinese Medicine, and its leaves are antibacterial as well as antiviral, and are even useful in the treatment of cancer. Woad has been used for fevers and for the treatment of highly contagious diseases and infections, including *E. coli*, salmonella, and pneumonia, though these uses are best left to medical herbalists. The dried leaves and roots can be taken as a tea or a tincture with more pleasant tasting herbs to make an effective remedy against influenza and other viral infections, including chicken pox, shingles, tonsillitis, laryngitis, and viral meningitis. Woad is so powerful that it can increase the effectiveness of antiviral vaccines, but it should be avoided if a person has any kidney issues, and it should never be taken for more than two weeks and, when treating serious illness, always with the knowledge of any healthcare professional. Use with caution.

Meadowsweet, Woad, St John's Wort Bundle

Magically, woad is an excellent herb to increase clarity, courage, direction, and to contact the warrior within. It helps with self-empowerment, the gaining of magical or shamanic power, increasing life force, and protection.

Foraging and Wild Sourcing

Wild magic is ecologically mindful and need-driven, rather than consumerist in its practice. Many of the gifts of the earth are finite resources, and we must be aware of the consequences of our actions whenever we forage or wild source. It is just as important to remember to tread lightly and never take more than is needed. In addition, in the UK at present, a great deal of land is private, and even those spaces with common access may not always welcome foraging for any reason. It is therefore important to be aware of the dangers of trespassing—seek permission where appropriate to gather even wild herbs. Of course there are still wild spaces, national parks, and plenty of areas where someone can gather herbs and plant resources for personal use without doing any harm or leaving any environmental impact. Equally, the ability to grow some of these plants for ourselves is increasing all the time, with wild flower and herb seeds available online, together with many fruit, seeds, and flowers of many trees and other plants, so long as we are careful where and how they are sourced. That said, the ability to gather wild herbs and other green gifts under a full moon is irreplaceable and adds much power to our magics, so long as we do no harm and take no more than we personally need.

It was once a vital skill for all humans to know the land they lived on, and when and where the things they needed could be gathered; it was a crucial part of living in balance with the planet for our hunter-gatherer ancestors. The same skills have always been essential for animals of every kind who must hunt their prey or find the best plants to eat. Below is a list of some of the more useful plants that can be found in the UK and most of northern Europe and America for food, practical resources, and magical uses.

A Note on Plant Identification

Always check multiple resources online or in books when identifying a plant, fungus, or tree, and continue to do so every time you seek to gather materials from that plant until you are more than 100 percent sure you can identify a specimen correctly *every* time. I advise checking with three different sources unless you have the most recommended, recent, and easily consulted book on the subject. Different photos pick up different details of a plant, and each specimen looks different from its brothers and sisters depending on the season, soil, position in relation to the sun, and a whole host of other factors. For this reason, you must take your time to correctly identify anything you gather. Not all plants are safe, and some dangerous plants look like safe ones—be careful and take every precaution, *never* guess. This warning is especially true of mushrooms, as the toxic ones are particularly harmful. Educate yourself on mushroom identification as thoroughly as possible, and if you are ever in doubt, don't touch.

Foraging Rules

Always correctly identify your plant—don't take chances.

Never strip a plant of leaves, berries, or whatever part you are using. If necessary, take a little of what you need from a few plants to do no harm. This may take patience, but greed and impatience are not wild.

With annual plants, take as little as possible of any flowers or seeds— they need them to survive.

Never pull up whole plants along verges or paths: it's bad behaviour and goes against most conservation principles and practices. What's more, it's also often illegal.

Roadside plants may have fumes from car exhausts, powerful weed killer, and other chemicals on them; always avoid using plants that may have been sprayed with anything…including dog wee!

If you gather seeds or nuts to re-sow, make sure you do re-sow them! Do not waste anything you gather.

A Forager's Calendar

Please note most of these plants are freely available in the UK and Ireland, as well as some parts of North America, but care must be taken to correctly identify each plant according to its scientific name.

Winter

- Chanterelle *Cantharellus cibarius* (edible)
- Chickweed *Stellaria media* (edible, medicinal)
- Fairy ring champignon *Marasmius oreades* (edible, medicinal, magical)
- Jack by the hedge *Alliaria petiolate* (edible)
- Juniper *Juniperus var.* (edible, medicinal, magical)
- Mistletoe *Viscum album* (magical)
- Oyster mushrooms *Pleurotus ostreatus* (edible)

Spring

- Beech leaves *Fagus sylvatica* (edible, magical)
- Chickweed *Stellaria media* (edible, medicinal, magical)
- Dandelion flowers *Taraxacum officinale* (edible, medicinal, magical)
- Fairy ring champignon *Marasmius oreades* (edible, magical)
- Hawthorn leaves *Crataegus monogyna* (edible, medicinal, magical)
- Hop shoots *Humulus lupulus* (edible, medicinal, magical)
- Jack by the hedge *Alliaria petiolate* (edible)
- Morel *Morchella esculenta* (edible)
- Nettle *Urtica dioica* (edible, medicinal, magical)
- Plantain *Plantago major* (medicinal, magical)
- Ramsoms *Allium ursinum* (edible, medicinal, magical)
- Sea beet *Beta vulgaris* (edible)
- Sweet violet *Viola odorata* (edible, medicinal, magical)
- Vervain *Verbena officinalis* (medicinal, magical)

Summer

- Black mustard *Brassica nigra* (edible)
- Blackberry *Rubus fruticosus* (edible, medicinal, magical)
- Blackcurrants *Ribes nigrum* (edible)

- Carragheen *Chondrus crispus* (edible)
- Chanterelle *Cantharellus cibarius* (edible)
- Dandelion flowers *Taraxacum officinale* (edible, medicinal, magical)
- Elderberries *Sambucus nigra* (edible, medicinal, magical)
- Elderflower *Sambucus nigra* (edible, medicinal, magical)
- Fairy ring champingnon *Marasmius oreades* (edible, medicinal, magical)
- Giant puffball *Langermannia gigantea* (edible, magical)
- Gooseberry *Ribes uva-crispa* (edible)
- Hazelnuts *Corylus avellane* (edible, magical)
- Heather flowers *Calluna vulgaris* (edible, medicinal, magical)
- Hop shoots *Humulus lupulus* (edible, medicinal, magical)
- Lime blossom *Tilia europaea* (edible)
- Morels *Morchella esculenta* (edible)
- Mugwort *Artemesia vulgaris* (medicinal, magical)
- Nettle *Urtica dioica* (edible, medicinal, magical)
- Plantain *Plantago major* (medicinal, magical)
- Ramsoms *Allium ursinum* (edible, medicinal, magical)
- Raspberries *Rubus idaeus* (edible, medicinal, magical)
- Redcurrants *Ribes rubrum* (edible)
- Sea beet *Beta vulgaris* (edible)
- Sweet violets *Viola odorata* (edible, medicinal, magical)
- Vervain *Verbena officinalis* (medicinal, magical)
- Wild roses *Rosa canina* (edible, medicinal, magical)
- Wild strawberries *Fragaria vesca* (edible, magical)

Autumn

- Beech nuts *Fagus sylvatica* (edible, magical)
- Black mustard *Brassica nigra* (edible)
- Blackberry *Rubus var.* (edible, medicinal, magical)

- Chanterelle *Cantharellus cibarius* (edible)
- Chickweed *Stellaria media* (edible, medicinal)
- Dandelion roots *Taraxacum officinale* (edible, medicinal)
- Elderberries *Sambucus nigra* (edible, medicinal, magical)
- Giant puffball *Langermannia gigantea* (edible, magical)
- Hawthorn berries *Crataegus monogyna* (edible, medicinal magical)
- Hazelnuts *Corylus avellane* (edible, magical)
- Hop fruits *Humulus lupulus* (edible, medicinal, magical)
- Jack by the hedge *Alliaria petiolate* (edible)
- Juniper *juniperus var.* (edible, medicinal, magical)
- Medlar *Mespilus germanica* (edible, magical)
- Mugwort *Artemesia vulgaris* (medicinal, magical)
- Rosehips *Rosa canina* (edible, medicinal, magical)
- Rowan *Sorbus aucuparia* (edible, medicinal, magical)
- Sea beet *Beta vulgaris* (edible)
- Sloes *Prunus spinosa* (edible, magical)
- Sweet chestnut *Castanea sativa* (edible, magical)
- Wild strawberry *Fragaria vesca* (edible, magical)

Making Herbal Oils

Foraged and home-grown herbs can be used in all sorts of ways. One of the most versatile is to make an herbal infused oil. Depending on the herb, the oil can be used for cooking, applying topically to the skin, anointing, or mixed with beeswax to make a salve or ointment.

You will need your chosen herb, a glass jar, and a good quality olive or other neutral vegetable oil.

Some herbs will need drying beforehand so the oil does not go rancid. For example, dandelion oil will go rancid unless the flowers are dried first. Others will sometimes go rancid, but if possible, using the fresh herbs is always best. Fresh herbs retain more of the nutrients and life force than dried and work best for magical uses. There are so many variables in crafting oil; even the weather can affect one herb more than another, so it's best to try and see what happens. Most herbs will work just fine, and others can always be gathered again for another try if need be.

Pick your herbs with great care; honour their spirit and thank them as you do so. Harvesting wild herbs at the full moon tends to work best, whereas digging roots is best done around the waning but not the dark moon.

Herbs Visible in Attractive Bottle of Oil

Pack the herbs tightly into your jar and cover with oil to the very top of the jar so there is no room for air. Screw the lid on tightly and leave in a sunny spot for at least two weeks or up to a month.

The herbs will gradually infuse the oil, which can then be strained. Store the oil in a dark glass jar or bottle, and label. Kept in a dark cool cupboard, it should last for at least a year.

To Make a Salve or Ointment

To make an infused oil into a salve, simply warm the oil over low heat and slowly melt in pure beeswax. Salves and ointments are useful, as its possible to mix several types of infused oil together and even add other ingredients such as essential oils and other dried herbs. For a harder salve, use about one part beeswax to four parts oil, use between two to five for a softer mix, less for a harder, body-butter type mix. When the beeswax and oil are fully melted, pour carefully into clean jars and leave to cool for several hours. Always label and include an ingredients list and date. Salves and ointments should keep for at least a year if stored in airtight containers in a place that is cool and dark.

Sacred Space Clearers: Herb Bundles and Saining Sticks

Saining, the Celtic tradition of burning herbs for sacred cleansing and healing purposes, has a long history. Juniper is the usual herb of choice, particularly in the more northern and mountainous regions, but other herbs may be used for the task as well. The usual practice was to close all the doors and windows and burn great quantities of juniper to fill the whole house with smoke. The doors and windows were then opened to let the fresh air in. At other times, the herbs were burnt in a censer and taken deisil (clockwise) around the house, or around the property. This option is more practical for colder, frequently damp climates. Similar to the use of Native American white sage in smudging, saining instead uses our own native plants and spiritual and geographical context. This is preferable for many reasons, least of which is that the herbs which grow in your own climate or landscape often resonate better with the spirits in your location. How we negotiate these matters when we practice Celtic spirituality but are not living in Ireland and the British Isles is a delicate matter, taking into consideration the sustainability of using various herbs and their cultural context; sensitivity and common sense have to both play their part, as does a good dose of tuning into any guidance we may receive from the spirits. Often, we will find the equivalents of certain plants all around the world, but each case needs individual consideration, with plants from our location perhaps used responsibly in tandem with those we purchase online from responsible sources. In practice, it seems everyone responds to the challenge of working with the Celtic traditions in other countries in different ways that depend on their local climate and situation, adapting in response to the practical and ethical concerns of their location to avoid cultural appropriation, and be as ecologically responsible as possible whilst retaining the spirit of the tradition.

Popular and effective herbs for saining from the Celtic tradition and the northern European climate are as follows, but some can be found in many locations around the world, or grown privately with care:

- Juniper
- Mugwort
- Lavender
- Rosemary
- Vervain
- Garden sage
- Mullein
- Yarrow
- Rose petals
- Lemon balm
- Scots pine
- Rowan leaves

❭ PRACTICAL ❰
MAKING A SAINING HERB BUNDLE

Gather your plants, and while they are still fresh, cut them to 7- to 10-inch lengths. Bundle them tightly, and roll them over and over, either upon a tabletop, or your leg, until they are have become a relatively compact shape. Take a pure cotton or hemp thread approximately four times the length of the herbs and wrap and tie the bottom of the bundle. Knot it so that you have approximately equal lengths of thread on either side. Holding the bundle tightly, criss-cross your thread, tying the bundle neatly from bottom to top and back again before securing tightly with another knot. Finally, place the bundles somewhere open and airy to dry; hanging in a window is perfect, as are placing them in a basket (so long as they are not over packed), or laying them on a drying screen.

To Burn

Place the bundle or hold it over a fireproof bowl or shell, as burning herbs can drop embers freely. Care must be taken for safety. Light the bundle at one end and waft it or blow upon it so you have glowing embers rather than open flame; a feather or hand fan work well for this. Then use the feather, fan, or your own hand to waft the smoke around your space. Pay special attention to corners, nooks and crannies, or areas where stuck or negative energy may accumulate.

Sage or Juniper Spray

An alternative to herb bundles is to make a spray, which can be used for energetic clearing when you need to ensure there is no smoke. The most popular choices for a clearing spray are usually either sage or juniper, but all sorts of herbs can be effective for this or chosen to add their own specific properties.

There are several effective ways make your spray. The first is to use essential oils instead of making your own with fresh herbs. The other methods rely on making herbal tinctures or tisanes/teas beforehand. Note that these are less fragrant but still retain the magical energy of the plant spirit.

You will need
- A dark glass spray bottle with spray attachment/cap
- Blessed spring water or distilled water
- A small pinch of salt/sea salt/Himalayan salt
- Drops of your chosen essential oil
- Vodka
- Quartz crystal chips (optional)

To make using oils

Fill the bottle halfway with the water, then add the essential oils, more than you would use for a message blend (perhaps ten drops for a small bottle). If you are using more than one oil, aim for a total of ten drops, or you may use ten of one type of essential oil. Add the salt and the optional quartz crystal chips to add some extra clearing energy to the spray, then top up the bottle with the vodka until full.

Hold it in your hands and bless the mix. Shake it before use to re-energise it and mix the oils afresh.

Tinctures and Tisanes

Herbal tinctures can be put immediately into your spray bottle and used as is, or you can add some salt or crystal chips as you prefer. You can also use a tisane, but its best to make a strong tisane and only fill the bottle halfway, topping it off with alcohol to preserve it.

It's also perfectly good to make a spray with a mix of essential oils, tinctures, tisanes, and vibrational flower essences. The main thing with a space spray it that it has a powerful cleansing energy, so it is important to use the correct herbs and bless it before use.

To Make an Herbal Tincture

Making herbal tinctures is easy: all you need is a jar with a tight-fitting lid, some vodka or other alcoholic spirit, and your herbs. Vodka or brandy are the most common choices.

Try to gather your herbs with as much care and respect for their indwelling plant spirits as possible and thank them for their gift.

Take a clean jar and pack your herbs into it before topping it up with vodka/ alcoholic spirit to the brim. The higher alcohol content the better, as this preserves the herbs as it draws out their properties. Seal the lid tightly and label with the herb, the name of the preservative, and the date. Leave in a cool, dark cupboard or the back of the fridge for at least two weeks, up to two or three months. Then strain the tincture to remove the herbal matter and place the liquid—it will most likely have changed colour to a greeny brown—in a sterile jar or bottle, dark glass is best. Again, label and date. Kept in a cool, dark place, the tincture should last up to two years.

To Make an Herbal Tisane

A tisane is very much like a normal herbal tea; the term is more of an herbalist or green witches' name for it. To make a tisane, gather your herbs (ideally fresh with due sacred care, but dried herbs work equally well), boil some water—fresh spring water is ideal but any water will do—and bless it before pouring it over either a sprig or two of the fresh herbs or one heaped teaspoon of the dried herb per mug of hot water. Leave to steep for five minutes before stirring it clockwise with a wooden or silver spoon to add a little more positive intention into the brew.

Flower Essences

Flower essences, also known as vibrational essences, are excellent magical tools that serve as a subtle yet powerful way of working with plant spirits of all kinds. The nature of flower essences is such that even quite toxic plants can be worked with for their beneficial effects quite safely, and their spirits can be worked with in a physical, tangible way without any risk. A flower or plant essence is the vibrational essence or pattern of the plant—in other words, its spirit—held in fresh spring water. Due to the spiritual and magical qualities of spring water, the energetic pattern of the plant and its spirit can be held in the water and carried around away from the plant itself whilst leaving the plant and its spirit unharmed and still connected. In this way, the plant spirit or vibration can work physically with the human body and overlay any illness or imbalance with its own energy to draw it back to health. It can also of course be used for many other purposes, such as helping the practitioner to clear a space when used in a spray instead of burning incense. When used in spell work, it can help manifest a desire, uncover hidden knowledge, or achieve a greater depth of wisdom. It can also be used to send healing and support to others at a distance, acting as a go-between ally. In this way, the plant spirits help you communicate with other spirits who are less close to your own vibration and may be harder to communicate with, such as those in a far deeper communion with the earth than ourselves. When we make our own essences in cocreation with our plant spirit allies, the possibilities for this kind of working become endless.

Humans have worked with plant spirits to make essences of various kinds for thousands of years, and examples of this kind of work can be found in Greek, Indian, and Chinese cultures, to name a few. Often the dew of the plant is gathered in the first rays of dawn, which is believed to be the most powerful and potent concentration of a plant's energies, but there are many ways of producing this kind of magic and plant medicine.

To Make a Flower or Plant Essence

When you've decided which type of plant you want to work with, you need to decide which exact plant and when are you going to make the essence. To make this decision, it's best to spend some time meditating or in communion with the plant spirit itself, asking its permission and advice using the methods discussed earlier. Some plants are best worked with when in full flower, others just before, so the time of year can have a dramatic effect on the essences you can make. Some plants do not have much of a flower to work with and should thus only be approached just before sprouting or at leaf unfurl; others are best to work with at their height in full summer. Common sense and a good connection with the plant should help you work out your timing. The next consideration is whether to make these in conjunction with the moon or the sun.

The Sun Method

Most flower essences are made using the sun method. Choose a sunny day when the plant is in full bloom, a clear glass bowl filled with fresh spring water, and a few of the blooms to place upon its surface. The water, the sunlight, and the plant work together to infuse the water with the plant's energy. This can take several hours, or the whole day. It may be best to begin the essence making process at dawn to benefit from the freshest solar energy and when the plant's energy rises to greet the new day, so that you work in alignment with this and gain the maximum benefit.

You may be occasionally directed to refrain from cutting or picking the blooms or leaves off; if so, simply pour the water over the plant, catch it in another bowl underneath, or leave the bowl nestled amongst the flowers, all of which are highly effective.

The Moon Method

More rarely, certain plants will be best worked with by moonlight—often, these are plants used for magical purposes, are night blooming, or are sacred to a lunar goddess. Making essences is usually then performed when the moon is full and is best done on clear nights when the light of the full moon feels brightest. On these occasions, the full moon and its energies can be invoked, the essence made within a sacred space and left to absorb the lunar energies as well as that of the plant spirit to work together vibrationally.

Even rarer are the times when combining the energies of a plant and certain stellar bodies are required, as with vervain, which is associated with the constellation of Sirius. Today we have all sorts of apps and maps to help us work out when a certain star is visible in the sky and to find it. When the particular celestial body is located, it can also be invoked and invited to send its stellar rays down to work with the plant in the same way.

Each time you make an essence with the plant spirit, the results may slightly differ as communication with the plant spirit informs you of what is needed each time. Always make the effort to thank the plant spirit, the spirit of the water, the sun/moon/stars, and any other intelligences involved in its making, and remember that you are working in a sacred manner.

Bottling and Preserving

When you feel your essence is complete and you have finished any cere-monial aspects to your working, bottle the essence in a dark glass (or sim-ilar) container to keep it cool and away from direct light. Alcohol can be added in the same amount as the water; e.g., 50 percent water and 50 per-cent alcohol, to help preserve it. Brandy and vodka are good for this, but glycerine and vinegar can also be used to preserve in this way if you prefer. Essences plus preservative can be stored and used internally for up to a year, although they can be used magically for far longer. Essences without any preservative can be used fresh, and so long as they are not taken internally, can be used indefinitely.

Seven

HONOURING THE SACRED LAND

At the heart of wild magic must be our connection to the landscape and its inherent spirit. Relating to the land where we dwell as a sacred, powerful being in its own right can both inform and empower our practice and vastly widen our perspective. With our perspective widened, we may position our lives in a wider and wilder ancestral context that takes us to the very sacred centre and source, vivifying and enlivening our spirits and all life around us.

Sacred Sites and Stones

We're lucky in Britain and Ireland that so many traces of our ancestors remain upon the land, etched upon the hills and valleys like the lines on their faces. From the early cave art by hunter gatherers at Creswell Craggs in Derbyshire of bison, reindeer, and birds, as well as symbols hinting at their spiritual beliefs that date back to the Ice Age, to our famous Neolithic henges, stone circles, and barrow mounds such as Stonehenge and Avebury, both World Heritage sites. Ireland as well is so rich in ancient sacred sites that connecting with our ancestral roots can come relatively easy. Every part of our long histories has left their mark in some way upon the land and

189

can be visited and explored. And just as the archaeology remains, so do the spirits, eternally watching over us as we seek to commune with these powerful ancient and sacred places.

While many of my students in other parts of the world believe that their local landscapes—especially those living in cities—no longer have a trace of their distant beliefs upon them, I find with a little detective work it is never truly the case. With a little digging—looking at histories and old maps, spending time meditating and seeking connection with the land spirits— the ancestral roots in an area and areas important to their spiritual beliefs can almost always be found. Sometimes this means seeking traces of indigenous cultures who lived in the area before the current civilisation; again, such knowledge may take a little research but can nearly always be found, and leads to a much deeper level of respect and connection. When contacting the spirits of place, the landscape, and its sacred sites, it is this deeper level of knowledge that we are looking for to ground our work. If there is an older indigenous culture where you live, it is their view of the landscape that will be the most useful. Make sure that respect, honour, and awareness are always applied to your exploration of these cultures. Information from the culture's practices can help you connect to the land around you in a way which would be impossible otherwise. Failing all else, maps especially are useful; noticing and tracking the waterways through a city, for example, can be highly rewarding and in time open a connection to the local gods and other beings. Often a natural spring or ancient well will have a history of veneration, and its residing spirits, as will any other important landscape features such as lakes, large rock formations, caves, hilltops, or ravines. Equally, not all sacred sites are human made or have a history of human veneration—they may be spiritual centres of the earth herself—sacred to the spirits, to the wild, without any human trace yet the air of blessedness and power emanates strongly from them all the same.

Once you have identified sacred sites in your area, build a relationship with them. This doesn't mean merely visiting as a tourist on a sunny afternoon but engaging in regular visits over an extended period at all times of day, seasons, and weather conditions, if possible, to give the place active care. *Giving* can mean many things, and while we may do rituals and other exercises to connect to the spirits of a place, we should never let ourselves fall into the trap of thinking that we and only we may know what a place needs or wants. For this reason, we should hold firmly in our mind that our first duty after or during building a relationship is to do no harm. Allow the site to reveal itself to you over time. Collect rubbish from the area, contribute to its care financially by giving to any charity that cares for the place, or engage with volunteer programs any organisations or caretakers of a site may run. But we must also take steps not to interfere with an area's biodiversity or archaeology. Take care to leave no physical trace behind—take only memories. The spirits remember those who care for a place without greed or seeking a return in some way, and will in their own time perhaps choose to draw closer to you or lend you their assistance with thanks. However, always remember this is kinship you are seeking to build, a relationship with mutual respect. One does not make friends by only coming to another when you want something. It is the same with sacred sites. See them often, and just be with them and the spirits within them, for the simple pleasure of connection. Let the opportunities arise for the land and the spirits to tell you how they want to be treated and what they need, if anything, from your relationship.

Sometimes it is not possible to physically visit a sacred site, and while making a physical visit and connecting with the spirits in situ is always preferable, connecting entirely via inner vision is also possible and can be very powerful. In this case it is useful to know the area already, or at least become familiar with it via photos or online. It is fine if you see details in your inner vision that differ from what is physically present, as what you are connecting with is its presence in the spirit realm rather than its physical presence.

Ways to Connect with Sacred Sites

Find a power place on the land near you and honour it as sacred, even if you feel it isn't. Clear away rubbish. Protect it from development and pollution. Make ceremony. Treat every living thing in an area as a miracle. Honour the seasons and her cycles of growth and rest by visiting at sacred times. Create or attend seasonal celebrations. Seek out archaeological and historical knowledge of an area. Mediate upon the earth. Journey to meet its guardian spirits. Feel the energetic flows on the land with your body. Learn to dowse. Give regular offerings to the spirits.

☽ EXERCISE ☾
CONNECTING TO THE GUARDIAN SPIRIT

When approaching sacred sites, it is important to remember that we may not be aware of the etiquette or rituals that the culture which built or originally venerated the site may have used. Equally, we may not be aware of the etiquette the spirits associated with that place and culture still expect; sometimes this is fine but in other places it can cause problems. We should never presume that our presence and behaviour at a site will not cause offence to the spirits. It is important to remember that when entering a sacred place of any culture, we are expected to behave in a sacred manner and conduct ourselves with sensitivity and respect, even towards beings we may not be aware of. For this reason, it is always important to go to ancient sacred sites of any kind with a gentle humility and to be as present to any sensations or intuitions we may have when we are there as these may be attempts to communicate with us. It is also vitally important that we ask the spirits permission to be there.

Most sacred sites will have a discernible, designated entrance of some kind; take care whenever possible to always approach a sacred site by using this entrance if you can, even if you arrive across open ground. When you come to the entrance, don't immediately enter—pause a moment to arrive and feel present within the place. Take a few breaths, look around to note what you can see from this viewpoint, and take heed of anything you sense or see—gusts of wind, birds in flight, or other omens. Take note of any physical sensations: how does your chest, stomach, or brow feel? Reach out to the sides of the entrance with your hands—can you feel any strange sensations? How about ahead of you or behind you? Take this opportunity to call in your own allies and guardians quietly. Nothing elaborate is needed here; make a simple call verbally or internally. Ask them to explore this place with you and take a moment to sense any guidance they may give you. Next try to sense the spirits of the place and its guardian or guardians. Regardless of what you sense at this point, ask permission to be there out loud before entering, and let them know that you come with respect and friendship. Use your own words if you can. I often use what follows or similar:

> Guardians and allies of this sacred site, 1 come in friendship
> and with respect, although I do not know your ways. Please
> may I enter your sacred enclosure?

Taking a couple of breaths, see if you sense anything—look for a clear *no*, as it will often be discernible if you're sensitive to it. If you don't sense a clear no, trust that you are probably fine. You may not get an answer, but the care you are taking will be noted and may help you later.

Next, I usually walk around a site, especially if it is a stone circle or long barrow in a circular, clockwise (or sunwise/deisil) direction, because it is commonly held to raise the power in a place, or at the very least doesn't wind down or banish the energy (which would be achieved by going anticlockwise/widdershins). I take care to greet and acknowledge any specific features in the place that seem particularly important or feel significant. If it's a stone circle, for example, I take note of and greet every stone; at other places I may take care to greet specific features that call out for attention in other ways, such as approaching or making a small bow to any large stone formations, or taking a moment to bow my head and look down into a holy well, or sacred spring, to show my respects.

After I feel I have taken in a sense of the place as a whole, I look out for where I feel its centre will be. It's easy to find the centre of a stone circle, but it takes more effort in other places; usually it's best to use a balance between common sense, a place's geography, and feeling, i.e., *where does its heart seem to be?* I then go to this place, settle myself for a while to tune in on a deeper level, and try to connect with the guardian spirit.

I connect with the guardian of a place by being as still and present as possible, taking some breaths and slowing myself down, and really feeling the place around me. I then enter a light meditative space and verbally ask for the guardian to come to me if they will. Again, I state that I come in friendship and with respect and state I would like to learn a little more about the place and how to connect with it in a deeper way. I make all these statements in a gentle, conversational way. At this point, I also tend to give an offering of something small and biodegradable, like a few flowers, or a little cream or whiskey poured onto the ground or placed in a simple bowl next to me. At other times, I sing a song or recite a poem. It all depends on what feels right and is responsible behaviour for the site. After a moment, I return to silence, and let my awareness open to sense the guardian. Sometimes I sense my spirit kin with me when I do this, and they help pass on messages and guidance. At other times, they sit further back and are not needed. Guardians of sacred sites, like other spirits, may take on any form, and the form they use may change, depending on many factors, but when I open myself up to connect with them, I have never failed to sense them and connect with them in a useful manner, no matter how ancient or abandoned the place may be. Even in places with dark or scary reputations, I have always managed to sense the guardian and have connected with them in a friendly and respectful way when working in this manner. Over the years I have come to the conclusion that it is showing these courtesies which has allowed me to steer clear of trouble and learn many things that would have otherwise been closed to me. That said, I always come with respect for myself also, being willing to call for assistance, and engaging from the point of view of a mutually respectful relationship. I will say no to sprits and politely leave if something is asked of me I do not agree to or if I feel uncomfortable.

Most of the time, a guardian will approach you as you sit in the sacred centre of the site, or you feel it is already there waiting for you. You can have really useful and insightful conversations—guardians often like to share what a place was used for and talk about the people who built it. At other times, they show me how to work with it in the present and perform spontaneous ceremonies with me or show me visions of the ancestors and how they perceived their world. At other times, I have been blessed to receive deep healing and communion with beings beyond my own comprehension. Every time is different, even at the same sacred site; just like every

Stone Circle

time you visit a loved one, your conversations will not repeat but sometimes continue where you left off. This is how relationships are built—by being open to the spirits of a place and minimising your own expectations and projections.

Ley Lines, Dragon Lines, Faery Roads, and Spirit Paths

Ancient cultures around the world maintained that the earth is covered in a vast network of energetic channels, lines of life force which crisscross the planet rather like the nervous system or veins of the body. These channels are often swift moving conduits for spirits, faeries, and other beings, and also have some discernible effect upon the atmosphere of an area. In Britain these paths are often called ley lines, or dragon lines. In Ireland they are often known as faery roads. The name *ley line* comes from an excellent and definitive book on the subject, *The Old Straight Track* by Alfred Watkins, who found alignments between sacred sites across the English landscape. These days, they are often called *dragon lines* in the UK; Watkins' leys were supposed to be a purely physical phenomena, but these alignments were also by and large powerful energetic currents along which dragons were thought to move, embodying the life force and ancient power and wisdom of the earth itself. In Ireland and more remote parts of the UK where traditional knowledge is still retained, they are called faery roads, as these are the paths faeries are said to take during their seasonal *rades* or rides, where they move from one location to another. Many faery raths or hollow hills—the hillforts and the round and long barrows (burial mounds) of our ancestors—were placed on faery roads. While the larger ones tend to follow the alignments of sacred sites across the country and even across the planet and can be tens of feet wide, they are in fact found everywhere; others can be quite thin and small. These sacred sites act rather like hubs or junction boxes, with lines meeting upon them and in turn spreading out across the land.

Like a vein or a nerve, these currents of energy tend to flow in a distinct direction, although when working with a dragon line it can be discovered that they also have undercurrents so to speak, which flow the other, opposite direction as well. When seeking contact with a dragon line in my inner vision, I was shown the image of a stick of rhubarb with striations, a line or cord of energy, with many other fibrous cords within it, each serving different purposes. It describes the anatomy of a dragon line very well.

Dragon lines or leys are fantastic to travel along while journeying or in your inner vision, and they are useful places to do magic, as you can harness the energy flowing towards you. They can also be worked with to take energy away, if they are willing. I tend to treat them as vast beneficent sentient beings; so far, it's worked well. For that reason, I ask the spirit of the dragon line to assist me, and I tune in to its guidance rather than assume it is there for my bidding.

While it is powerful and very informative to work with dragon lines, it's not a good idea to live on them or sleep upon them, as they tend to drain the life force from someone. This is the prime cause of geopathic stress, or sick building syndrome, where their flow or lack of it around an area can have profound effects on those who live there. However, when flowing as intended and undisturbed by human buildings or underground works, they can be very positive for animals and plants. Some animals run along the routes of a dragon line, while others are reluctant to cross them and avoid them as much as they can, perhaps due to the intensity of the energy. Large trees, especially ancient oaks, appear to flourish along dragon lines; like sacred sites, they serve as hubs or meeting places for these energies. They are excellent places to meditate and contact the spirits for this very reason.

Dowsing

Many people can sense or feel dragon or ley lines, and it is generally good to spend some time developing the sensitivity using your body to dowse and notice energetic changes if you can. Begin by sensing how your solar plexus feels throughout the day, notice when it feels comfortable and when it feels anxious or tense—a lot of dowsing with the body can be developed from this core awareness. Gradually you can also start to ask yourself questions and notice how your solar plexus feels when you consider each option, or the nature of what you feel, as well as general yes or no answers.

Other useful ways to sense dragon lines is to try traditional dowsing using either L shaped copper rods, or a forked hazel stick. Working with a pendulum to find them is also effective.

Dowsing rods are simple to use, and it is best to not overthink it when you work with them. Hold them steady, with your elbows bent and arms raised in front of you to chest height. Keep the long end of the rods parallel to the ground and to each other, about a foot apart. Walk in a gridlike pattern around the area; in places of energy, the rods will cross. You'll feel it quite distinctly and clearly enough that it's disturbed many a sceptic over the years! After a while, you will build up a pattern of the lines of energy around a space, and it is possible to fine tune your dowsing by asking the rods to show you dragon lines, underground water passages, areas of stuck energy, and even the location of spirits or lost items. Remember that it is not the rods that have the answers, it is your body and inner knowing, which is far harder to access without some help. The sensation that it is something separate from you is still very clear—after all, it *is* separate, your infinite self as opposed to your day-to-day mind which answers.

Something similar occurs when using a pendulum. Pendulums don't have to be special objects made of crystal or metal; a ring on a chain or a piece of string works just as well. The only requirement is that it is able to hang freely about a foot or so and be weighted at one end. To use a pendulum, be clear on your *yes, no, sometimes,* and *maybe* responses before using it. It is simple to do this: It is simple to do this: ask the pendulum to confirm something you know the answer to (such as your name) to get your yes or no. Next ask something else you know the answer to for the maybe and sometimes, such as "Do I like rainy days?" or even "what is the movement for maybe? For most people a *yes* is a clockwise circle, and *no* an anticlockwise circle, but it can differ. After you've done this a few times, you'll get a sense of its patterns and it can become quite useful.

That said, while working with dowsing rods and pendulums can be great fun and very effective, the best way will always be to be able to feel things with your body and be aware of what your body is telling you- in many ways that can be a spiritual quest in and of itself!

Mapping Dragon Lines

A great deal of information is available online about dowsing and tracking dragon or ley lines across the landscape. To this end, a great many excellent maps have been made of key energetic lines across the country, and the world, particularly those which touch on sacred sites such as Stonehenge or Glastonbury Tor. It is possible to find dragon lines without any form of dowsing whatsoever simply by examining a detailed map of a large enough area and finding a place where three or more sacred or important energetic sites form a line. These can take any form, from notable hilltops—often called beacon hills in the UK—to stone circles and standing stones, to churches and very ancient trees. In some places such as Washington, DC, it has been well documented how government buildings have been positioned to deliberately form alignments in this way.

Take a large map, a pencil, and a ruler, and see if you can discern any alignments in your area, likely spanning several miles, or more. You can then use your inner vision, or a pendulum to see if these alignments have any discernible energetic feeling about them.

) PRACTICAL (
DRAGON PATH JOURNEY

Try this exercise to travel along a dragon line or faery path in your inner vision; see what you encounter. You will first need to have identified a dragon line but do not need to be physically with it or near it for this inner working. You do, however, need to know its physical location, and the direction it flows and its axis, e.g., northwest to southeast.

Begin this exercise by asking your guides, allies, and any other good spirit beings you work with to accompany you. Sitting comfortably but not lying down, take three deep breaths. Feel your feet firmly on the floor and your body fully present to your position on the land at that moment, the feel of the chair beneath you, and the feel of the room or space in which you sit.

Set your intention by verbally stating that you wish to explore the dragon line you have in mind and ask it permission. You may or may not sense its indwelling spirit at this time, but allow it a space to communicate with you, and see how you feel in your belly. Do you have permission to proceed?

Visualise the line where you know it to be: see yourself in your inner vision approaching it. You may see it as a thick band of flowing golden energy snaking its way across the land.

When you feel you have a clear sense of it in your inner vision, step into the line and let its current carry you. You will find that you can cover large stretches of the landscape quite quickly, and that sometimes you will be above the ground by several feet or more, able to look down at the land, at other times, you will move through it as if you flow under the earth itself. Be aware of any physical sensations you feel as you fly along its current, and any details that come to you of buildings, hilltops and rivers, any geographical detail that presents itself. These may be the same as in the everyday world, or quite different, symbolically expressing some different message about the land and its condition, as well as the function of the line itself. See if you can get a sense of the dragon line as a spirit and get a feel of its purpose and nature. If you are able, ask it about its experiences and what it is like to be a dragon line. Ask if it will show you some of the ways in which you can work together to heal the land when needed.

After some time has passed, step off the dragon line at a building or some other notable location. Do you know where it is in our terrestrial, physical realm? If visiting won't invade anyone's privacy, have a look around and then return to the dragon line with the intention of returning home. Zoom back along the line until you come to the place where you started. Return to your everyday consciousness by breathing deeply and feeling the air in your lungs and the pulse in your veins and in your chest. Wiggle your fingers and toes, and feel yourself back sitting up. Slowly open your eyes. You might want to record your experiences in a journal.

Paths of the Dead

Paths of the dead can sometimes be the same thing as ley lines and dragon lines, and similar to faery roads, in that they are energetic currents that run over the land. However, they can also be distinctly different, as their main purpose is to carry the souls of the dead to the otherworld. These paths are sometimes the same tracks people in remote areas use to transport their dead to church for burial. It's a common tale in Celtic lands for people to see their loved ones walking along the dead road or the path of the dead through the wild countryside, sometimes interpreted as a vision or omen that their loved one would soon die. Such paths are often called *dead* or *dodd lanes*, in addition to other local variations, and it is surprising how many of these paths are still marked and named as such in our modern villages and towns; a sign of their importance lingering into the present day. It is never good to live on a dead lane, but they are useful and play an important role in the spirit world. Once connected to such a road, a soul cannot get lost and is carried gently to their next destination, accompanied by those who have gone before them.

If great care and respect are shown, paths of the dead can be worked with to help spirits or those who are lost pass on by directing them to travel this way to meet their loved ones within your inner vision. It is also useful to work with these when a space needs clearing, and unwelcome spirits need to be sent on their way, as the current of energy will not let them return, but will lead them to the care they need in order to heal and transform.

Going on a pilgrimage along the paths of the dead is a good way to remember ancestors and those who walked the land before you, whether they are of your bloodline or not. Sharing tales of your bloodline in such a place is also very powerful, and it sends healing to those on your line. Placing a lantern (safely and responsibly) or a biodegradable offering to be cleared up carefully after a set period of time upon a dead road or a crossroads leading to one is a good way to honour the spirits each Samhain or when a loved one dies. But do not spend too much time in such places— while you may see many ghosts and interesting phenomena, they are not healthy places for the living.

Faery Roads

Like dragon or ley lines, faery roads and some paths of the dead are energetic currents across the earth. Some faery roads fit all three definitions, while others will be reserved for the faeries only. Remember that these faeries are not the twinkly pixies of Walt Disney—they can take much less cutesy forms and are members of powerful spirit nations of the British Isles, and as such command great respect. Their nature is distinct from many other types of spirit; I advise not spending too much time on devising definitions and linear categories for the faeries or any other spirit, as experience will fox you every time … they defy such limitations! But when one has felt the presence of faery, there is no mistaking it, and it is never forgotten.

Faeries are often said (especially in Scotland) to move along faery paths during their quarterly migrations, while others choose them as the route for their faery rades or rides. Equally in Ireland the trooping faeries, *an slua sí,* are said to regularly travel along particular routes laid aside just for them. Such paths often go from faery fort or rath to faery fort, or along a line of hollow hills or burial cairns, and through faery thorns- sacred hawthorn trees. It is taboo to ever disturb a faery road in any way, by effecting anything on its route. All faery thorns, raths, forts, or other faery locations should always be left unspoilt or untampered, lest the faeries exact their terrible revenge. Ireland in particular has many tales that date well into our current age about harm that has come to those who have damaged a faery road including untimely death, sometimes for several generations.

It is possible to track faery roads by dowsing, and using the sensitivity in your body, as well as exploring them in vision accompanied by your guides and allies. In the mortal everyday realm, these paths can pop up and disappear somewhat randomly, leading off cliff tops or into rivers; they can also take strange routes that zigzag or spiral across the land seemingly at will.

A good thing to try is to sit near a faery road, at the sacred times of the cross-quarter days, Imbolc, Beltane, Lughnasadh, or Samhain, at dawn or dusk. Make an offering to the land and the faerie spirits of cream, honey, or something you have baked. Sit in silence and let your inner eye rest and see what you may experience. Sometimes the faeries are more felt than seen; for others they are heard, passing by in a great rush sometimes with the sound of bells. For those with some experience, it is possible to seek a faery ally upon a faery road, if you are careful, polite, and ask at the right time. Sometimes in your inner vision you will see them coming towards you along the road, as if rushing in from afar. If you feel someone has been taken by the faeries (usually something that happens in spirit, like a form of shamanic soul loss), it is possible to travel with your faerie allies if you have protection along these roads in search of them. They can be called back to their mortal lives along these roads, just as it is possible to leave the mortal realm forever by travelling upon their currents.

Vigils and Vision Seeking

There is a popular Welsh tradition that on the summit of Cader Idris is an excavation in the rock resembling a couch and that whoever should pass a night in that seat would be found in the morning either dead, raving mad, or endowed with supernatural genius.[56]

---

56. R. Askew, *Bye-Gones, Relating to Wales and the Border Countries* (1884). https://archive.org /details/byegonesrelating1878unse/page/68.

There is an ancient practice across the Celtic lands of seeking vision in sacred sites and sitting in vigil. Usually these places are high mountain tops; there is also mention of barrow mounds or other liminal places noted for their spirit presence in some way, such as riversides or holy wells. There are examples of similar practices in other lands, such as the Native and South American traditions of vision quests, where a seeker sits out on the land and fasts for several days in search of a vision. The traditional Celtic examples differ slightly from these, however. Records of the Irish *Filí*, oracular poets and seers who were the last keepers of the ancient druid traditions, show us that they would seek darkness and sensory deprivation in order to receive a vision, such as in the ritual to decide the next king, the *Tarbh Feis*. There was also a ritual to seek an answer to a problem or create an oracular poem, *Imbas Forosnai*. However, the latter would usually be performed indoors, in a purpose-built ritual shelter, perhaps constructed due to the colder weather in northern Europe, as well as the importance of immersion in the earth when seeking ritual darkness in a way those working in the barrow mounds would have experienced thousands of years before. The Celtic practice of vigils outside appears to have always been for a shorter amount of time, such as overnight- the task being to encounter the spirits more than experience the limits of your physical endurance, although total immersion in nature is essential.

Sitting in vigil (from the Latin *vigilia,* meaning *wakefulness*) means to purposefully set aside time in which to honour or acknowledge something as an act of devotion or spiritual communion. A vigil is a conscious enforced period of presence, dedicating your time, body and awareness to a single sacred purpose. In the Celtic traditions this purpose is to primarily honour the powers of place within the landscape, to sit in a state of constant and yet unexpectant communion with the land, to breathe together, to be as one, for the purpose of relationship alone. The results of a vigil on the land may be profound and life changing; they may equally be quiet and subtle. It may be something a seeker practices many times, regularly or sporadically, or just once depending on a host of circumstances and the individual's path.

When we think of vigils and vision quests, it is important to be clear what sort of practice we are discussing, and why it is done. This is not the same as a camping trip—it is instead about entering a space where your inner self and the spirits come into close contact, and your consciousness is changed. Here we are seeking transformative experiences for healing and self-knowledge, for contact with our own souls. The vision we may receive (if we receive one), may take all sorts of forms. In this practice, we are allowing space for the spirits to contact us and for our deep self to make itself know to us. In many ways, vigils can be considered pilgrimages to the self and the heart of the land; two become one, effects can be profound.

One of the most famous places to seek vision is the top of Cader Idris, in Wales, and there are other sites in Scotland, England, and Ireland that have been used for this practice. Another Welsh example is *Maen du'r Arddu (the Black Stone of Arrdu)*:

> In a stony place, called Yr Arddu, Black Ham, pretty high in Cwm brwynog farm, on the ascent of Snowdon hill, there is a very large loose stone, called Maen du yr Arddu, i.e. The black Stone of Arddu; upon the top of which there is another lesser stone, seemingly as if it had been raised there by hands.
>
> It is said, that if two persons were to sleep a night on the top of this stone, in the morning one would find himself endued with the gift of poetry, and the other would become insane.
>
> And accordingly it is affirmed, that in a frolic two men, one called Huwcyn Sion y Canu, and the other Huw Belissa, agreed to sleep on the top of it one summer night: in the morning one found himself inspired with the celestial muse, and the other was quite bereaved of his senses.[57]

---

57. William Williams, *Observations in the Snowdon Mountains* (1802), 31-32. https://books.google
    .co.uk/books?id=h2w9AAAAYAAJ&pg=PA149#v=onepage&q&f=false.

In this excerpt, we see the ancient practice of exchange: for something to be attained, something must be sacrificed. The example of Yr Arddu is interesting, as it is the only one to mention two people, and that only one may return with wisdom, while the other suffers- the teaching here is two-fold, that there are always risks in seeking vision, in seeking to commune with those things beyond our everyday awareness, and that the results are never guaranteed. This tale may be seen in another way, too: for the seer or poet to emerge, some other part of us must die or be broken down to dust; the creation of an expanded consciousness depends upon the destruction of the previous limited world view. This doesn't mean that the risks are only metaphorical, however; for some, the costs really are too high, and this is not a practice for people who are very vulnerable in some way. At some point in life, we are supposed to be content and sheltered with hearth and home, leaving the wild ones in the hills for another day.

For this reason, I recommend this practice only be performed when you are in robust health physically, mentally, and emotionally; common sense must always be applied to all matters and there is *no* exception to this. Practical issues of safety must always come first. So be sure you fully know the area you will be in and are able to assess its dangers and resources. Have all the equipment and supplies you need and be sure that you can effectively carry them when necessary. Ensure that people know where you will be and for how long (for women especially, don't post your location to strangers on social media but *do* tell friends or relatives) and that you have a phone and appropriate extra charge for it as well as a sensibly equipped medical kit. We must always respect the danger of the wild first and foremost, even in our search to befriend it.

Practicalities aside, if we enter sacred communion with the land for an hour, a night, three days, or a week…the spirits will see that we receive just what we need and are ready for in that moment. The aim here is not to re-enact vision quests from other cultures, but to tune in to the land you are on, and the blood in your veins, and see what they say. Every act of vigil is sacred and powerful, large or small.

Central to the idea of vigil is that of connection and observance, to be as deeply present to the land, the gods, the spirits, as possible, without the distractions of daily life and our everyday consciousness. Often this is done by simply creating the space, and allowing it to be filled by forces and presence beyond ourselves, such as by sitting in silent meditation and contemplation; at other times, this connection may be grown by making prayers and other sacred acts of ritual and ceremony.

I have sat in vigil many times in my life. Some have been large scale, epic occasions; other times they have been simple and all-too-brief interludes in a busy life. But every vigil has been a time of deep soul nourishment and the cultivating of inner vision and connection. It is impossible to truly engage with the practice of vigil and not emerge knowing oneself a little better, at the very least. To spend time in the presence of your own awareness and how much or little you can access something more profound beyond your daily inner dialogue is very revealing. At best, it allows a dynamic awakening to life's profundity and the position of your soul in the midst of an infinite spirit world; at the least, it allows you a space to become aware of how hard you may find it to leave your daily concerns behind, in turn providing fuel for attempts at a later date. Either way, you return to the normal world with a greater awareness of yourself and the great infinite *All* that lies just beyond.

Prayers and Offerings

There are many ways to make prayers and keep your intentions clear when doing a vigil. Prayers can be in any form—the possibilities are endless. Here are but a few:

Creating a sacred space with circle casting, meditation, silence, chants or drumming. Lighting a ritual fire, keeping an eternal flame. Giving offerings. Invoking specific spirits or deities. Dancing and other ritual movements, perhaps with the spirits, ancestors or with animal allies and familiars. Drawing or walking labyrinths. Breathwork. Drawing and painting. Making ritual objects. Writing poetry and free form writing to give voice to the land. Playing live music or singing to serenade the spirits. Reciting poetry. Creating mandalas. Reciting lists of your ancestors. Clearing an area of rubbish. Ritual cleansing with herbs, water or smoke. Planting trees and tending the green kin of an area. Making herbal medicines and biodynamic potions to heal land and people. Holding space for others and passing on their prayers to the land.

Before any of these, however, the best way to relate and perform a vigil is to be open to letting the land and your spirits inform what you do. Arrive and just be for a while. Listen and let your inner voice and the spirits themselves guide how you should spend your time. This includes just sitting and waiting, side by side with your own inner workings, doubts and impatience, until you are able to move beyond them. This is a powerful practice all by itself.

The very act of performing a vigil can be an offering in and of itself- and is a strong step towards building a relationship with the deeper aspects of your own life, as well as with the numinous forces that surround us.

Seeking Guidance

It is perfectly sensible to ask the spirits how they feel you should perform your vigil, including when and where. Divination techniques, such as ogham, tarot, or other tools can be useful here. Shamanic journeying or communing with your spirit allies in other ways if you feel you can do so competently, are also excellent ways to seek out how they would like to work with you. Techniques such as fire scrying and *néladóracht* (cloud divination) can also be helpful. It may be that you have no fixed idea of what you should do during your vigil or even why to do one, other than feeling this is something to try, and that is fine too. Creating a space and opportunity to grow a closer connection is an important and sacred task in its own right; it allows the voice of the spirits and your own inner promptings to be heard.

Herbs for Opening Perception

There are many herbs and other natural substances that have been used for thousands of years to help induce visions and spirit guidance. Ingested as teas and potions, smoked and burnt as offerings—to list them all here would be impossible, and while some of their effects are undoubtedly powerful, they may be too powerful for some and as such must be used with the guidance of experienced practitioners steeped in their culture and use. There are many gentler herbs that can be used legally and effectively not to induce hallucinogenic visions but function as spirit allies to guide and stimulate the practitioner's inner world, help with psychic work, in scrying and meditation, and to induce visionary dreams. Such herbs and herbal mixes also make good offerings to the spirits.

Visionary herbs that are safe to use include

- Angelica, *Angelica archangelica*: protective, useful dream guide
- Betony, *Stachys officinalis*: protective against nightmares
- Chamomile, *Chamaemilum nobile:* meditative, protective
- Hazel, *Corylus avellane:* inspirational
- Lavender, *Lavandula angustifolia*: protective, cleansing, relaxing
- Mugwort, *Artemisia vulgaris*: visionary (mild psychotropic, always avoid in pregnancy)
- Sage (especially *Salvia divinorum):* very short-lived but mild psychotropic to strongly hallucinogenic effects depending on dose; always use sparingly and be aware of any legal issues in your locale) or *Salvia officinalis.*
- Wormwood, *Artemisia absinthium*: protective, visionary (avoid in pregnancy)

☽ PRACTICAL ☾
VISION BREW

This gentle brew is a good place to start with using herbs for seeking vision. It is safe and can be used to aid meditation and lucid dreaming, and it makes inner guidance during divination more easily accessible. Feel free to omit any ingredients and add others as you choose. As always, use common sense and awareness of any safety issues if you have any health conditions.

- 2 tsp mugwort
- 1 tsp angelica
- 1 tsp hazel leaves
- 1 tsp sage
- 1 tsp lavender
- 3 tsp mint (for taste and to ease digestion)
- Honey to taste

Combine the dried herbs in a pot and pour over 1 litre boiling water, preferably freshly boiled spring water. Steep for at least 10 minutes, longer if possible. Try one cup at a time. The rest can be stored in the fridge for a day or two.

Mugwort is an *artemesia*, named after the goddess Artemis and is sacred to the moon. For the best results, steep overnight somewhere where it will be touched by moonlight to charge up with her power and to bless it to increase its potency and effectiveness.

❯ PRACTICAL ❮
TENM LAIDA: ILLUMINATION OF SONG

Throughout this book have been several mentions of offerings of song. These can be simple everyday songs you love, that raise your energy, and send your feelings out as an offering. They could also be deeply meaningful songs or chants, such as ones you have created or heard before. The Irish oracular poets, known as the *Filí*, who used their art in search of divine inspiration using animist approaches performed a technique called *Tenm Laida,* which means *illumination of song.* These may be spirit songs or chants which have come to you through inspiration during your meditations and other practices, or they may come to you in the moment, as part of your ritual or magical work. Central to much of the earlier Celtic magical practices was the idea of receiving inspiration, literally meaning *to receive the breath of the gods,* to become "inspirited."

There are many ways to do this practice, but it does not come easily to everyone; time needs to be taken to hone and practice your skills and get your creative juices flowing. Equally, its fine to allow yourself to simply speak or sing out of the blue, and allow time to get a tune or a rhythm developing organically (although, don't expect great chants to come out of the blue). Allow the words to find their way into the world with patience and a childlike, playful attitude.

A good way to do this, is to just start allowing yourself to make simple noises. Hums and intoning, or vowel sounds are a good place to start. Don't wait for it to be perfect to begin, give yourself permission to just make a noise, let it be as quiet or as loud as you choose, and treat it as if it doesn't matter, its just a beginning. Slowly, casually, let a rhythm build up, just of noises, as you would with a baby or a small child.

The Irish word for inspiration, *Imbas,* is a good word to chant or intone. Allow plenty of playfulness with the *mmmm* and *sssss* sounds. The Welsh world for inspiration, *Awen,* also allows for some lovely round vowel sounds, as well as the *nnnn.* Play with these words and all the sounds you can make out of them. Over time, you will find that a beat or a tune begins to develop on its own. Get out of its way and just play, let some other part of your mind make the song, while you let your awareness just float for a while. This is your spirit song, made by and for you by the spirits themselves; it cannot be repeated, as everyone's is different. The song will become your truest expression, a great offering of connection beyond words between you and the spirits, the gods, the *All* that surrounds you. It can become like a river of sounds, beginning somewhere beyond our awareness, out in infinity, pouring out from the Source, out into the mortal world and taking shape there as pure spirit. It may happen every time, it may happen once in a hundred tries, but every attempt is a perfect offering to the spirits around you, and to the gods—it aligns you and gives them a voice, enriching everything with their vivifying touch.

☽ PRACTICAL ☾
CENTRE THE COMPASS
SIMPLE VIGIL RITUAL

At no point should anything you read in a book take precedence over a clear message of what to do from the spirits. Rituals are always best performed in close communion with the spirits and the land or location in which they are performed. Every vigil, no matter how long or short, simple or complex, will be performed in a different way by different people and in different places. Being fully present to yourself and to the spirits where you are should always be the prime focus. That said, a simple template to work with can provide a useful guide to get you started which you can then adapt and evolve, or abandon, as you see fit. The following simple ritual is intended in this way, as a format for you to grow your own practice from or in response to as your relationships with the land and the spirits develop.

Presuming you have already chosen the site of your vigil and are familiar with its history, relevance, and geographical details, and that you have taken all practical common sense measures into account, you can weave your own ceremony when you begin to open it as a sacred space for the purpose of your vigil or work there. If it is an ancient sacred site, then it is already sacred of course, but setting up a basic sacred space helps to set your intention and somehow frame what you are doing there. It also provides a framework to make an offering and make your connection to the place more conscious and deliberate. It casts a circle deisil (sun-wise), in line with energetic cycles of life on the land and the turning of the earth, it also honours the three worlds of earth, sea, and sky, the sacred triplicity of the Celtic traditions, to orient us within a sacred and honoured landscape.

Begin by cleaning and clearing the place of any rubbish—sadly, this is an often-needed task all around the world. Taking some responsibility for the care of the place is an excellent first step. Next, take a moment to orient yourself and take note of the four directions, the four *airts* in later Scottish Gaelic practice.

Prepare your offering: in this instance a gift of incense, or of a good drink like whiskey or mead work well, as do milk or cream. You could also offer a piece of homemade cake or bannock, or the gift of song. Note that any offering will need to be repeated or divided into four parts.

Turning first to the east, greet the place of the rising sun and all the land and sky about you to the east. Honour it in your own words, or try what follows as a template:

> Winds of the east and all that lies before me here! I honour you and give thanks to you!

Now place your offering upon the ground, cast it into the air, or sing with all your heart to the east.

Now turn to the south. Greet the place of summer's warmth and all the land and sky about you to the south. Honour it in your own words or again, try what follows as a template:

> Winds of the south and all that lies before me here! I honour you and give thanks to you!

Again, place your offering upon the ground, cast it into the air, or sing with all your heart to the south.

Turn now to the west. Greet the place of the setting sun, and all the land and sky about you to the west. Honour it in your own words or what follows as a template:

> Winds of the west and all that lies before me here! I honour you and give thanks to you!

Again place your offering upon the ground, cast it into the air, or sing with all your heart to the west.

Finally, turn to the north, the place of the cold winds of winter, and all the land and sky about you to the north. Honour it in your own words, or use what follows as a template:

> Winds of the north and all that lies before me here! I honour
> you and give thanks to you!

Now again place your offering upon the ground, cast it into the air, or
sing with all your heart to the north.

Now look up to the sky and contemplate the vastness of the sky and
space above you. Bow your head or acknowledge it some other way. Again,
using your own words or what follows, speak out loud your prayer to the
realms above (known as *Gwynfed* in Welsh and *Albios* to the ancient Gauls;
both words mean *white, light,* or *blessed*).

> I honour the realms of sky above, of Albios, of Gwynfed, the
> seat of the sun and stars!

Look or kneel down and turn your attention to the ground beneath
your feet. Look around you at the good earth and all the living things that
surround you, known as *Abred* in Welsh and *Bitu,* or *the world of the living
beings* in Gaulish. Again, speak out loud your prayer to the realms of earth:

> I honour the realms of earth, here with me, of Abred, of Bitu,
> land of the living!

Now turn your attention to the far horizons. Remember the sea and
ocean that surround the land on this blue planet of ours. Consider its vastness and its great depths. Consider the water within you and the depth of
your own eternal being, at one with the great sea of being. Again, using
your own words, honour the realms of sea and the underworld/otherworld
of the Celtic tradition known as *Annwfn* in Welsh, and *Dubnos* in Gaulish,
both meaning *the deep place*.

> I honour the realms of sea below me, of Annwfn, of Dubnos, I
> honour you the place of depths beyond measure, within me
> and beyond!

Finally stand still. Feel your own heartbeat within your chest, your feet upon the earth, and your head beneath the sky. Feel yourself at the centre of things, positioned within your own centre. Take nine deep slow breaths, feeling yourself truly here, present and in contact with this immediate point of time, and point on the land. Again, use your own words or try these to get started.

> Spirits of this place, here and now: I honour you, I am with you! May all my time with you be a living prayer!

Leave this "circle" open—do not bid the four directions or the three worlds goodbye until you have completed your vigil. Instead, let them now inform and orient your time, setting your vigil in the landscape that surrounds you and the cycles of the day and night and seasons that colour it.

Person Cross Legged in Vigil by Standing Stone

Before you leave your vigil, return to each of the three worlds and four directions in reverse order to thank them for being with you. Again, using your own words is best, but a simple *I thank you north, west, south, and east! I thank you, sea, earth, and sky, for being with me here! May you be blessed!* is sufficient.

CONCLUSION

We live in times when our need to honour the wild and reconnect with the natural world is greater than it has been for several generations. As a species, we must all remember that we are part of a vast and interdependent network of living spirit, seen and unseen. Physically, psychologically, and spiritually, none of us are truly alone; we are all but drops of consciousness, infinitely beautiful, shimmering on an endlessly heaving sea of being. We are still, under our layers of modernity, as we were meant to be—wild souls, sparks of the divine, powerful living spirits, each a part of the sacred living earth, inseparable and whole. As the modern world pulls us away from remembering the earth herself as sacred, so we need to honour her all the more and strive to reinvigorate our lives and souls with her elemental nourishment. If we can remember the myriad of beings around us, seen and unseen, even for a short time each day, we nurture the seeds of magic within us and the saplings of our spiritual growth. It is possible for us to return to a time of miracles and wonders, where the ruin of the last centuries can be healed and our relationship with our spirit cousins, brothers, and sisters of all kinds may flourish again. Every tree grows from a single seed; every forest, a single tree. Every act of wild magic is an act of communion and empowerment that restores our connection with something greater than ourselves. You are wild, you are magic, you are one of many.

Be blessed.

BIBLIOGRAPHY

Caesar, Julius, W. A. Macdevitt, trans. *The Gallic Wars, De Bello Gallico* (Latin and English). US: Neptune Publishing, Kindle Edition, 2012.

Carey, John, Katja Ritari and Alexandra Bergholm, eds. "The Old Gods of Ireland in the Later Middle Ages," *Understanding Celtic Religion: Revisiting the Pagan Past*. Cardiff, Wales: University of Wales Press, 2015.

Carmichael, Alexander. *Carmina Gadelica* volume 1. Originally published 1900, Edinburgh, Scotland: T. and A. Constable. https://www.sacred-texts.com/neu/celt/cg.htm

———. *Carmina Gadelica* volume 2. Originally published 1900, Edinburgh, Scotland: T. and A. Constable. https://www.sacred-texts.com/neu/celt/cg2/index.htm.

Campbell, John Gregorson. *Superstitions of the Highlands and Islands of Scotland*. Originally published 1900, Glasgow, Scotland: James MacLehose and Sons. US: AlbaCraft Publishing, Kindle Edition, 2012.

Campbell, John Gregorson. *Witchcraft and Second Sight in the Highlands and Islands of Scotland*. Originally published 1902, Glasgow, Scotland: James MacLehose and Sons. US: AlbaCraft Publishing, Kindle Edition, 2012.

Courtney, Margaret Ann. *Cornish Feasts and Folk-Lore*. Originally published 1890, Penzance, UK: Beare and Son. US: AlbaCraft Publishing, Kindle Edition, 2009.

Hull, Eleanor, ed. "The Saltair Na Rann," *The Poem-book of the Gael*. Originally published 1913, Chicago: Chatto and Windus. https://archive.org/details/poembookofgael00hulliala/page/4.

King, Graham. *The British Book of Spells & Charms*. London: Troy Books, 2015.

Lucan, Nora K. Chadwick, trans. *Pharsalia*, book I, lines 450–62 in *The Druids*. Cardiff, Wales: Cardiff University Press: 1966.

Mackenzie, Donald. *Scottish Folk-Lore and Folk Life: Studies in Race, Culture and Tradition*. Originally published 1935, London, Blackie. US: Obscure Press, Kindle Edition, 2013.

Martin, Martin. *A Description of the Western Islands of Scotland*. Originally published 1703, London: Printed for Andrew Bell, at the Cross-Keys and Bible in Cornhill, near Stocks-Market. AlbaCraft Publishing, Kindle Edition, 2013.

O'Grady, Standish Hayes, trans. *Agallamh na Senórach*, in *Silva Gadelica*. Originally published 1892, London: Williams and Norgate.

Pliny, John Bostock, trans. *Naturalis Historia*. Originally published 1855, London: Taylor and Francis, Red Lion Court, Fleet Street. http://www.perseus.tufts.edu/hopper/text?doc=Perseus%3Atext%3A1999.02.0137%3Abook%3D1%3Achapter%3Ddedication

Pitcairn, Robert. *Ancient Criminal Trials in Scotland, 3*, part 2. Originally published 1829, Edinburgh, Scotland: Bannatyne Club.

Editors of Edinburgh University Press. *The Scottish Antiquary, or, Northern Notes and Queries* vol 7. Originally published 1893, Edinburgh,

Scotland: Edinburgh University Press. https://www.jstor.org/stable/25516556?seq=1#page_scan_tab_contents.

O'Rahilly, Thomas F. *Early Irish History and Mythology*. Dublin, IE: Dublin Institute for Advanced Studies, 1946.

Siculus, Diodorus, Francis R. Walton, trans. *Library of History, Volume XI: Fragments of Books 21-32*. Cambridge, MA: Harvard University Press, 1957. Reprinted for Loeb Classical Library 409.

Spence, Jr. John. *Shetland Folk-lore*. Originally published 1899, Lerwick, Scotland: Johnson & Grieg. AlbraCraft Publishing, Kindle edition, 2013.

Wilby. Emma. *Cunning Folk and Familiar Spirits: Shamanistic Visionary Traditions in Early Modern British Witchcraft and Magic*. Eastbourne, UK: Sussex Academic Press, 2013.

Williams. William. *Observations in the Snowdon Mountains*. Originally published 1802. https://books.google.co.uk/books?id=h2w9AAAAYAAJ&pg=PA149#v=onepage&q&f=false.

Wunn, Ina. "Beginning of Religion" in *Numen* 47, no. 4 (2000): 435–436. http://www.jstor.org.ezproxy.uwtsd.ac.uk/stable/3270307.

Webpages

Irish Archaeology. "The sweat house at Creevaghbaun, Co. Galway." http://irisharchaeology.ie/2012/03/the-sweat-house-at-creevaghbaun-co-galway/.

archive.org. "R. Askew, (1884) Bye-Gones, Relating to Wales and the Border Countries." https://archive.org/details/byegonesrelating1878unse/page/68.

Carhart-Harris, Robin, Leor Roseman, Mark Bolstridge, et al. "Psilocybin for treatment-resistant depression: fMRI-measured brain mechanisms." *Scientific Reports* 7: 13187. https://www.nature.com/articles/s41598-017-13282-7.

sacred-texts.com. "The Child Ballads: 113. The Great Silkie of Sule Skerry." https://sacred-texts.com/neu/eng/child/ch113.htm.

INDEX

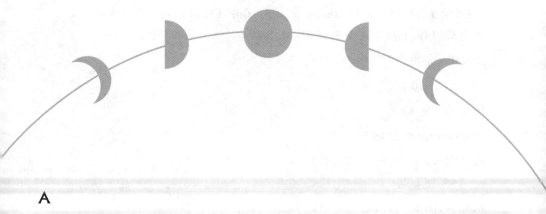

V

W